THE STORIES FOR
My Grandchildren

KRESIMIR BANOVAC

Brilliant Books Literary
137 Forest Park Lane Thomasville
North Carolina 27360 USA

To my grandchildren
Anna, Nick, Luka, Lauren, Lia and Theo

CONTENTS

MYTHOLOGY

I have already told you some of these stories, and you loved to hear them, some of them several times. So knowing that, and having more time nowadays I decided to wrote some of mythology stories for you.

Somebody long time ago wrote – "Do not say these stories are too beautiful to be true. They are too beautiful *not* to be true".

Although the stories are over 2000 years old their grace and freshness make them as magnificent today as they were then.

I selected these stories from Greek mythology hoping that they might stimulate you one day to read the others that are not included here.

APOLLO AND CLYTIE

Clytie was a pretty girl who showed her affection to Apollo, God of Sun but he became more and more indifferent. So she began to slowly leave him. All her thought was for the god of sun and her gaze was ever upon him. She gave no care to herself, taking neither food nor drink, caring not about her clothing, hair or her appearance.

In time she died. But her limbs became rooted in the ground, her body changed to a slender trunk, and her head became a flower. But, unlike other flowers Clytie's head moved on the stalk. She always turned her head to the sun, looking at the east in the morning and at the west in the evening.

And Clytie became the sunflower that turns on to her God at sunset and looks at him again at the sunrise.

ATALANTA AND HIPPOMENES

While Atalanta was still a child, an Oracle told her that her marriage would be fatal to her. So she made up her mind never to marry. She avoided all communication with men and lived in the woods devoted to hunting and sports.

Yet she was so beautiful and many men approached her as suitors. At last Atlanta called them all together and announced that she would become the bride of one who could bit her in a foot race. On those who failed, however, would be imposed the penalty of death.

A number of them announced their readiness to engage in the contest. All of them failed and ended up with cruel penalty.

In one race, in which she was engaged, a certain young man, Hippomenes, acted as a judge. He said that no girl was so beautiful or desirable as to be worth the hazard of death.

Yet when he saw the graceful form of Atlanta, running as lightly as a bird and when he gazed upon her face as lovely as that of a goddess, he changed his mind, and was eager as the rest to win her.

Hippomenes eagerly approached her and challenged her to race. Atalanta looked at him and felt sorry, for of all the young men who had contented with her none pleased her better than Hippomenes.

Hippomenes was smart. He knew that he couldn't win the race so he prayed to Goddess Venus to help him. Venus heard him, and listened to his prayer. She went to garden and gathered three wonderful golden apples and gave them to him with some instructions how to run.

The next day the race took place, both runners flashed from the start like arrows. Despite his best efforts, Hippomenes saw the girl take the lead. Then he threw into the path of Atalanta one of the golden apples. Its beauty dazzled her eyes, and without realizing what she was doing she stopped and snatched it from the ground. As she did so, Hippomenes overtook and passed her. But again she passed him, and again a golden apple fluttered into her path. Again she paused to pick it up and once more gave Hippomenes the advantage. But her speed was so great that in a few moments she led the way again. Now the end of the course was near, and in desperation Hippomenes threw forward the last of the apples. It rolled out of the of the truck, and Atalanta hesitated, deciding whether or not to stop to pick it up. But the wonder of the apple was so great that she turned aside and stooped and lifted it from the ground. As she did so, Hippomenes had won.

Atalanta was not altogether sorry to become the wife of Hippomenes, but her Oracle was yet to be fulfilled.

Both lovers were so happy that they forget to give gratitude to Venus, from whom the victory of Hippomenes had come. Angered at their forgetfulness, the goddess changed them to beasts – Hippomenes to a lion, Atalanta to a lioness.

CALLISCO AND HER SON

Callisco was a woman who had handsome son. Goddess Juno was jelous and very angry on Calisco and changed her to a bear. Callisco was very sorry in the woods and dared not to mingle with the other bears for she fear of them and yet she fled from the hunters, since naturally they would try to catch her. One day, she saw in the distance her own son. Her love was so great that she approached him with clumsy gait, she stood on her hind legs and sought to embrace him. But he draw back in panic and as the bear persisted in following him he raised up his spear and was about to kill the strange but terrifying animal. However, God Jupiter looking down from the heavens, saw what was happening and in pity stayed the spear of her son. Then Jupiter changed both of them into the stars and put them in the heaven. We can see them today, one group of the stars we called Great Bear; Callisco, and nearby is the Little Bear, her son.

CIRCA AND ULYSSES

I am sure that you remember story about Trojan horse. The man who gave Greeks the idea to build a wooden horse was Ulysses. He was one of the Greek warriors and was a very smart fellow. But in Greek mythology Gods were often divided, and not all of them liked what Ulysses did to people of Troy. They punished him to sail back to Greece with his crew and on the way home to have many obstacles.

One big problem for Ulysses was when he met one-eyed Cyclopes who lived on an island with sheep. You remember this story and a happy end. Ulysses saved his live and lives of his sailors with a smart trick.

There were several other places on his trip to home where Ulysses needed to think how to survive. Here is one of the stories.

After long sailing Ulysses and his crew were very hungry and thirsty. They were very happy when they found an island. On the island lived alone a girl Circe who spent her time in studying magic. She learned all sort of tricks and became so clever that she could turn men into whatever beasts she liked. When strangers landed on her island, she changed them to lions and wolfs and pigs. Her garden was full of animals, which wandered back and forth. After sailors drop anchor in the bay they started wading ashore for water and food. Ulysses stayed on the ship and sent a leader with his men. On the island was a palace and when they came to the entrance Circe open the door and invited them to enter. The leader of the group was smart, like his boss Ulysses, and stayed outside while his men went inside to eat and drink. When the men had finished eating and drinking they stretched themselves on the benches to rest. Then their hostess Circe took a little magic stick and touched them very lightly, one by one. At once long ears began to spring from their heads and before their leader knew what was happening, his friends had vanished and in their stead a group of grunting pigs wadded around the palace. He ran back to the ship and told the others what had happen. Ulysses was very angry and wanted to go at once to the island and save his men.

We do not know what would have happened to Ulysses if God Mercury were not there at that time. He told Ulysses - however brave you may be your sward would not overcome the magic of Circe. But if you carry this little green branch in your hand, it will keep you save from her magic.

Ulysses entered the garden, the beasts crowded close around him and followed him to the entrance. Circe herself came to meet him, much pleased to have another victim. She smiled as she watched him eat and drink, thinking what a fine big pig he would make. But when she touched him with her magic stick nothing happened the power of little green branch turned her magic aside. Ulysses drew his sward and rushed at her, commanding her to release his friends. Circe was so frightened that she knelt before him and begged him to spare her. She promised to free all her prisoners. Circe kept her promise and changed back all animals to people, gave Ulysses water and food and said good-bye to them.

This time Ulysses was very lucky, it was not him but God Mercury who outsmarted this girl's magic.

Now at the end of the story let me ask you something.
Would you like to have her magic stick?
Whom you would touch?

DWELLERS IN TARTARUS

Tartarus was Greek Underground or Hell. The Gods sent there as you know only bad guys.

Here are the stories about two of them. The first one is Tantalus.

Tantalus was a rich man while alive, and the Gods had given him many favors, but in spite of this he committed many grave crimes, even killing his own son.

When he died, he was ordered by Gods to suffer a never-ending punishment.

He found himself standing in clear water that barely touched his chin; and right above his head there hung branches of all kinds of fruit.

Tantalus, constantly tortured with hunger and thirst, sought ever to sip the water and to grasp the fruit. But it was always in vain – always the water receded from his lips and the branches moved away from his grasping hands.

Today people often say for some things that are impossible to finish – This is "Tantalus' torture".

The other story is one of the favorites of Nick and Luka. It is about Sisyphus.

He was the king of Corinth. He was very good in sailing and trading but was also a man of greed and fraud.

On his death he was punished to roll uphill a huge marble block. When, after endless and bitter pushing, he reached the top with it, the stone immediately rolled back to the bottom of the hill, and Sisyphus had to begin all over again.

Today we also used to say for hard things
to do – "Sisyphus Work".

ECHO AND NARCISSUS

Echo was a beautiful nymph who was the special favorite of Juno, Goddess of Heaven. But one day Juno discovered that Echo had purposely refused to talk to her. In anger Juno punished Echo by taking from her power of conversation – Echo could only repeat what someone else said to her. This was an annoying punishment.

One day a handsome young man, named Narcissus, happened to wander into the woods that Echo visited. Echo immediately fell in love with him, but when Narcissus spoke to her, all she could do was to repeat his words.

Narcissus thought that she was making fun of him and did all he could do to avoid her. But everywhere that he went Echo followed him and all what Narcissus said she could just reply by repeating to him what he had just said.

In despair Echo faded away until she was no more than a voice – a voice that still lives in caves, cliffs and desolate places, and repeats what you say.

What happened to Narcissus?

He, however, not only repelled Echo – he also repelled all the other girls, for he believed nobody is quite good enough for him.

One girl finally prayed to Gods that he might have the experience of knowing what it was to love and not to be loved in return. Her prayer was granted in a most curious way.

Narcissus, bending one day over a mountain pool to drink its cooling water, saw his own image in the waves. Immediately he fall in love with the image, he talked to it, spoke of love, and finally reached over to embrace it – but all in vain.

So, like Echo, he stayed over there looking at this face in the water until he died.

But from his body sprang a flower that still bears his name – narcissus.

HERCULES

Hercules served a king who did not like him and gave him 12 difficult tasks to do.

This are 12 adventures of Hercules.

Hercules was very strong man; even as a baby he strangled two serpents in his cradle.

The first task was to slay a monstrous lion. Hercules had two weapons, tremendous club and arrows. He tried hard with his weapons but at last he strangled the monster to death with his hands.

The second task was to kill the nine-headed serpent Hydra. The problem was when he stuck off one head with the club 3 new heads grew immediately.

After a while he started to use a torch to burn the neck without the heads and like that he won.

The third task was to capture a wonderful stag with golden antlers. It took him a year to find the animal; he captured it and carried it to the king.

The fourth task was to kill a monster boar that was killing people in the mountains. Hercules caught it in a huge net and gave it to the king.

The fifth task was a fanny one. Hercules was supposed to clean the filthy stables of 3000 oxen not cleaned for 30 years. He went to the river and dug a wide ditch from the river to the stables and thoroughly washes them out.

The sixth task was to kill very greedy birds that like to eat human flesh. Hercules used a big rattle to make a great noise and scared the birds into flight. Then he slew them with his arrows.

The seventh task was to capture a bull.

The eighth task was to bring wild horses.

The ninth task to get a girdle from the queen of the Amazons, the women warriors.

The tenth task was to kill three-headed oxen that lived in an island far away of Greece.

The eleventh task is my favorite one. Hercules was supposed to fetch the golden apples guarded by a dragon in a garden. Hercules knew that near the garden lived Atlas, a mighty Titan who bore the weight of the heavens on his shoulders. Hercules asked Atlas if he would like to rest from the weight of the sky and stars. He offered to take the weight of the heavens on his own shoulders if Atlas would agree to go to the garden and bring him some golden apples. Atlas was so happy to be released from the burden of the sky and the stars and promised to do anything Hercules wished. So Hercules took the weight of the sky on his shoulders and Atlas stepped out, shouting and jumping with happiness to be free. He went to garden to get apples. Hercules held the heavens until Atlas finally returned with golden apples. He was afraid that Atlas might never come back and asked him to hold the sky a little until he rested his shoulders. He then set the sky again on giant's shoulders and went back to king with golden apples.

The last task was to bring three-headed watchdog Cerberus from the Underworld. He did not kill Cerberus but showed it to the king and sent it back to Underworld.

HYACINTHUS

Apollo was the God most beloved by the Greeks; he was protector of men – especially when children were engaged in sports and contests. Son of the king of Sparta named Hyacinthus was one of the favorite boys with whom Apollo liked to play. They went together fishing and hunting and participated in many sports.

God of the wing Zephyrus was equally fond of Hyacinthus and tried to win his favor, but the boy cared only for Apollo.

One day Apollo and Hyacinthus began a game with discus. Both were skillful players, and now one, now the other made the farther throw.

Unnoticed by either of them, Zephyrus was watching them and was very jealous and angry that Hyacinthus preferred Apollo to him. So he could not endure it no longer and when Apollo throw his discus it whizzed through the air but Zephyrus changed its course and sent it with deadly force toward Hyacinthus. The heavy missile stuck the boy in the head.

Apollo tried hard to revive the boy as he lay dying. He took boy in his arms and gave him promise of immortal life as a delicate flower. In shape like the lily but purple in color sprang from the ground.

The Greek called this flower the hyacinth, today we called it iris.

MIDAS

Midas was a king in a Greek city. He was very reach man. One day he went to a magician who told him that he would grant him any favor he wanted. Midas was very surprised with this offer and begged magician "Let all I touch be changed to gold". He was already fabulously rich, but he wanted still more.

And what happened now is a big surprise.

Everything Midas touched including food and water and even his beloved child became gold. He could not eat, drink nor touch his family. Finally in desperation Midas prayed to Gods and begged them to take his gift back.

The Gods commanded him the bath in the river, and when Midas did so, the curse was removed. But ever since that time river has had abundance of gold in its sands.

PROMETHEUS AND PANDORA'S BOX

These two stories are usually told together, start with a story about Prometheus, a Titan, and continue with a story about a beautiful girl with a special box.

Prometheus was God's child with many brothers and sisters. Boys were called Titans; they were big, tall and strong. (Tennessee football team players call themselves Titans, I am not sure they are so strong as Greek Titans).

Some of them were good Titans; the others were bad often making troubles. Prometheus was one of the good Titan.

As you would expect, Titans came on earth before people. Prometheus knew that the people were soon coming to live on Earth. As a good man he spent most of his time making things ready for their coming. He planted seeds; open little streams in the mountains to get water and watched over the animals. Prometheus was so nice that he thought that all these things were not enough and decided to give people a special gift. He was thinking about that for long time what he could do. At last he remembered the fire of the Gods. There was no fire on the Earth but man could use fire a lot, to cook, warm himself and to frighten away wild animals.

But how can he get fire?

Only Gods have fire, which was very high over the clouds close to the Sun.

He made a plan; he will get a long torch, go to High Mountain and try to reach the Sun's fire. One day when Gods were busy with something else he caught fire and went down the mountain as fast as he could.

He had fire for people. Zeus, the main God, did not like what Prometheus did. He was very angry with Prometheus for stealing fire for people. After people received from Prometheus stolen gift, Jupiter decided to punish them both.

In mythology we will see that Gods and Goddess are mainly good to people but sometimes they can be very rude.

How will Zeus punish Prometheus?

Zeus ordered to chain Prometheus to a rock on the mountain and sent an eagle every morning to bite and eat his body, which each night grew back again. That was a terrible punishment for a good Titan lasting for long time. He was chained in the mountain until a brave man called Hercules came to free him.

Zeus was not very happy when he heard what happened but he let them go and thought that Prometheus was punished enough.

This is the end of first story. It ends up with an action of Hercules who was the greatest Greek hero.

What was the punishment to the people?
Here it starts the second story.

Zeus ordered that a beautiful girl takes a big box to people. Her name was Pandora. The box was carefully sealed and was not supposed to be open.

Pandora came with the box to a Titan who told her not to open it. Pandora was very curious and one day she could not resist and opened the box. At this moment all the evils and troubles, worries and diseases flew out. She tried to put led back again but it was too late.

However one spirit remained in the box – Hope. A little creature told Pandora "You can never be altogether unhappy, Hope will always be near you to give you a comfort". Now we only have Hope that these bad things will not happen to us.

O, Pandora, Pandora what have you done!!!!!!!

I hope you like these two stories; we have not told them before. You will hear more, read more and see many pictures of

Prometheus and eagle. His only crime was to be nice and for which Zeus punished him so hard.

Was Zeus right to punish him for stealing fire?

You might say yes or no, for me it was hard to be a judge.

After reading about Pandora's box, remember not to be too curious, just a little bit is OK, "but not too much, because something may happen", we have read that also in Otto Fish book.

THESEUS

Theseus was a Greek hero. He lived with his mother and grandfather. His father was a king and left the home to rule the country. Father's name was Aegeus. Before he left home he told his wife not to tell his name to their son if he could not more a huge rock that he left next to the house.

Several years later Theseus had no a problem removing the rock, underneath he found father's sword. Now mother told him father's name and that he was a king of Greece.

Theseus wanted to meet his father. It was far to go to the king. He needed to go through many dangerous places and to meet many dangerous creatures.

However, Theseus was one of Greek heroes and like the others, he was strong, big, smart and good-looking.

I will not tell you about all enemies that Theseus needed to fight on his way to his father, but I will tell you just one, about Procrustes.

Procrustes was a bandit. His name means "he who stretches".

What was he doing, and why he was so dangerous? Procrustes had a house by the side of the road. He offered to passing strangers a pleasant meals and a very special bed. After the meal, he would take his guest to the room where was a very special bed. He told the guest that this bed should exactly match his size. As soon as guest lay down Procrustes started to work on him. If the guest were too short he would fasten chains to his arms and legs and stretch him until he was just right.

If the guest were too tall he would chop off his legs.

What a terrible man!

Procrustes "the stretcher" was a man who needed to be punished.

I hope that you all agree with me and Theseus.

Theseus did that for us. He had a plan.

Theseus asks Procrustes to show him how to lay down in this very special bed. As soon he was down in bed, Theseus stretched him real good and then he killed him.

That was the end of Procrustes and the end of Theseus' travel. The next stop was father's palace.

When Theseus came to father's palace his father immediately recognized his son who had his sword. Both of them were very happy.

But the king had a big problem. In an island next to father's city was a monster that was killing people. Monster was half-man, half–bull, called Minotaur. He lived in the center of a maze called Labyrinth. The Labyrinth was a maze that once inside, one never can find the way out again. Sooner or later, whoever enters would be face to face with Minotaur.

What Theseus did?

He had a plan.

He took a ball of thread and tied one end of the ball to the doorpost and went inside Labyrinth. While going inside more and more he kept unrolling the ball. He was lucky. He found Minotaur sleeping. Theseus used his strength and broke off one of Minotour's horn and stabbed him with it.

That was the end of monster Minotaur.

Theseus then followed the thread back to the entrance of Labyrinth.

His work on this island was finished and he went back to his ship to sail back to father.

He promised to his father to come back with white sails if he survived, but he was celebrating too much on the ship and forgot to change black sails.

When king Aegeus saw black sails on horizon he throw himself off a cleft into sea.

We call today this sea after him – Aegean Sea.

It could have been a happy end, unfortunately some mythology stories are big tragedies, but we still like to hear them over and over again. You will also see that sometimes Greek heroes needed to be cruel and punish bad guys.

This is the end of story about Theseus.

P.S.

English word "procrastination" was made after Procrustes. We use it when somebody is delaying, postponing or "stretching" to do work.

PERSEUS AND MEDUSA

Perseus was a grandson of a Greek king. An oracle of the Gods told king that his grandson will kill him. So he decided to get rid of him and commanded Perseus to and fight Medusa.

Medusa was a fearful creature, one of three sisters whose hair were hissing serpents, who had wings, brazen claws, and enormous teeth, and the most dangerous a glance that turned anyone to stone.

Perseus knew that by himself he could do nothing to Medusa so he sought the help from goddess Minerva and messenger Mercury.

They supplied him with three things – the helmet of Pluto, which made him invisible, a pair of winged sandals, which enabled him to fly with the speed of wind, and a highly polished shield. This shield was so shinny that it was like a mirror.

In a cavern at the island lived the sisters. When Perseus reached them they were asleep. He did not dare to look at Medusa directly but when Medusa got up, Perseus holding his shield in front of him walked slowly to her.

At that moment, Medusa looked at the shield and saw her face, she immediately turn into a stone.

So when the two other sisters awoke, the magic helmet of Pluto rendered him invisible and he escaped in safety. At the end monster Medusa defeated herself with the with her own weapon.

THE GREEK MYTHOLOGY STORIES ABOUT CUPID

C upid was the baby son of Aphrodite (Romans called her Venus). She was Greek goddess of love.

One day when Apollo, the God of light and sun, was driving his chart, Cupid followed him around, for he was more found of Apollo than of any other Gods. He was much interested in Apollo's bow and arrows and wanted to have his own.

Cupid asked Apollo "Give me one of your arrows. I'll do anything you say if you will only let me hold your bow". But Apollo laughed, and taking Cupid's hand, led him back to mother.

Cupid was greatly disappointed and decided that if he could not have Apollo's bow and arrows he would get some for himself.

He knew that Vulcan, the God of fire and blacksmiths, could make them for himself. So one day he asked Vulcan for a bow like Apollo's and some golden arrows. Vulcan made a little bow and quiver full of small golden arrows.

Now Cupid was happy. He was so delighted with his bow and arrows that he played with them from morning until night.

Mother Aphrodite watched him playing with the new toys, and she gave these small golden arrows a supernatural power.

When any one was touched even so lightly by one of the golden arrows, he at once fell in love with the first person he saw.

From here on, I will tell you three wonderful stories of Greek mythology about Cupid and his "Love Arrows".

The first story is about Apollo and Daphne.

The second story is about Pluto and Persephone and,

The third one is about Cupid himself and Psyche.

APOLLO AND DAPHNE

One day Apollo did not drive his chariot, but left it in the heavens behind the clouds.

"It is a good thing," he said "for people to have some free days". So he spent the day hunting in the forest. In a little glade he saw Cupid playing with his bow and arrows. Apollo was not happy and said "Put these down and leave such things for grown people".

Cupid was hurt and angry and said, "Your arrows may kill animals but mine shall wound you". As he spoke he let fly an arrow, which stuck Apollo so lightly it barely scratched him. Apollo laughed at him and walked on, not knowing what the wound really meant.

Soon he noticed a beautiful girl gathering flowers in the forest. Her name was Daphne. Apollo had often seen her before, but had never seemed so beautiful to him as now.

He ran forward to speak to her. She was very shy and when she saw him coming she ran away. Apollo wanted so much to be with her and talk to her that he ran more after her. Poor Daphne, terrified, ran faster and faster. When she could not run no more, she cried loudly to her father Peneus, the God of rivers, for help.

Peneus hearing his daughter's voice thought that she was in some terrible danger. Her father sent a magic power over the forest to protect her changing Daphne into a tree.

When Apollo reached out his hand to touch her, the beautiful Daphne had vanished. In her place stood a laurel tree.

He was so sad and stayed by the tree all afternoon, taking to the tree and begging Daphne to forgive him. He asked for some of her laurel leaves. Daphne shook her branches, and a shower of leaves fell around Apollo. By this he knew that Daphne forgave him, and he gathered the leaves in his hands and made a wreath.

Apollo placed this laurel wreath on his head, where it remained forever fresh and green.

This is the end of the first story about the magic arrows of Cupid.

The next story will take us to Greek's mythological Underground.

PLUTO AND PERSEPHONE

Pluto was the God of Underground. A dark, misty and gloomy place with no sunshine, no light except the glow of fire. In some places were dark caverns, caves and deep dark lakes. Pluto thought his kingdom is the most beautiful in the world.

Pluto seldom went to Earth because did not like the light of the sun and earth flowers and trees.

Cupid saw him once when he came to Earth, he drew his bow, and wounded the God of darkness with one of his arrows.

Pluto had just to turn back home, when he saw Persephone. She was beautiful. Her mother was the Goddess of harvest and loved her daughter a lot.

Persephone was dancing and gathering flowers when the God of dark kingdom grabbed her by the wrist, said nothing at all, but lifted her in his arms and took her to Underground.

Persephone screamed for help. She cried to mother Ceres but nobody could have helped her as Pluto carried her away.

Her mother Ceres was despaired, climbed mountains and crossed rivers asking everyone for Persephone, but neither men nor Gods would tell her were Pluto carried her daughter.

Exhausted of the search for her daughter, mother went to Zeus, the main God and said "Never again the leaves on the trees will be green, blue sky will be gray, and a cold wind and snow will swept over earth, unless my daughter is returned to me. Never again will I watch the harvest and men will die from hunger".

Zeus feared that Ceres would do as she threatened, so he sent Mercury, the speedy messenger, to Pluto to bid him to release Persephone.

Pluto and Persephone saw Mercury approaching and went to see him. Mercury said Zeus wants Persephone back to the Earth and to her mother. But Pluto had grown to love Persephone dearly. He could not bear to lose her forever, yet he wished her to be happy.

So Pluto agreed to let her go to her mother for six months of the year, but the other six months she promised to spend with him.

When mother got her daughter back, the bare branches burst into flowers and tiny green leaves. With Persephone return, Spring came back on Earth.

Wasn't that another mythological beauty?

But this story also tells us why we have every year, the six months nice weather, Spring and Summer, and the other half of the year, rainy months of Fall and icy Winter, when the beloved Persephone goes back to her husband in Underworld.

This is the end of second story.

The last story about Cupid is the one that I like the most. It is a story about wounded Cupid by his magic arrow?!

CUPID AND PSYCHE

Once there lived in Greece a princess named Psyche. She was beautiful, that strangers came from faraway countries to look at her. Even the Gods were delighted as they watched her from the heights of Mount Olympus.

Goddess of love, Aphrodite, was jealous and angry on Psyche. So she called her son Cupid and sent him to wound Psyche with one of his gold arrows. Cupid flew down to the palace where Psyche lay asleep. At once Psyche awoke and turned her eyes toward Cupid, although she could not see him, for he was invisible. Psyche was so pretty that Cupid's heart beat wildly and a weakness came over him such as he had never felt before. His hand slipped and he wounded himself with his own arrow.

That moment Cupid fell in love with Psyche.

He flew back to Olympus and told mother how Psyche was beautiful. Now Aphrodite was even angrier with Psyche then before.

She forbade Cupid to ever enter the palace of Psyche or to look upon her again. She also turned all of Psyche's lovers away from her.

Soon Psyche's sisters were married to great princes, but no young man sought Psyche.

Her parents very concerned went to oracle to seek advice and were told that a monster was waiting on her on the top of the mountain. They took Psyche to the mountain and at the top they bade her good-bye and left her alone.

She was weeping and trembling with fright. Zephyr, the west wind, came and lifted her gently in his arms and carried her to a wonderful white palace.

For long time Psyche did not see the monster of palace. He visited only in the night time, going away before morning, but his voice was gentle and tender, not at all like that of a monster.

Psyche sometimes begged her husband to stay through the day, but he always refused.

Psyche next asked her husband that her sisters might visit her. At first sisters were happy to see their young sister and find her safe and happy, but soon, seeing the entire splendor in Psyche's palace they became jealous.

Before they left they begged Psyche to look at Cupid, as he lay asleep. At midnight, when the lord was sleeping, Psyche arose, lit the lamp and bent over his couch.

The light showed her, not a dragon nor a monster, but a youth more beautiful than any she had ever seen. As she turned to put out the lamp, Cupid awoke and surprised, spread his wings and flew out of the window.

At this moment the palace and gardens vanished, and Psyche found herself again in her own home.

Day and night, without food or rest, she wandered to seek her husband. After long travel she found him and both of them were happy again.

Now Cupid flew to Jupiter and begged that Psyche might be immortal so that she might stay with him forever. Zeus granted Cupid's plea and sent Mercury to carry Psyche to Mount Olympus, where Gods were waiting to welcome her.

Ever after, on the sunny summit of Mt. Olympus, Cupid and Psyche lived together in happiness.

I hope you liked these three stories of love and beauty. Again and again they show, how wonderful is Greek mythology.

It was fun to write for you some mythological stories. Maybe I have already told you some of them, but now you will have them in a written form. I know that you like to read.

As you know there are many more stories in the Greek mythology, however, this is only my small selection of the numerous beauties.

To make sure that the stories are sufficiently decent for the young ladies, I gave them to your grandmother to read and we got her approval.

OEDIPUS AND THE SPHINX

Oedipus was the son of a Greek king. When he had grown up he left his hometown and came to the city of Thebes. He found the place in deep distress. For the city was being harassed by a terrible monster called the Sphinx—half-lion and half-woman—who stopped every passing traveler to ask him a riddle. If the traveler could not provide the right answer, the Sphinx killed him on the spot. But Oedipus, fearlessly, approached this intimidating monster to receive the riddle in his turn.

"What creature is it," the Sphinx asked him, "that in the morning goes on four feet, at noon on two, and at night on three?"

"Man," replied Oedipus without a moment's hesitation, "for it is he who creeps on hands and feet as a baby, stands on two feet when grown, and leans on a cane in old age." Bitterly disappointed at being thus bested, the Sphinx flung herself off the cliff to her death and was the danger of passers-by no more.

APHRODITE AND ADONIS

One day Aphrodite, the goddess of love and beauty, was playing with the arrows of her son Cupid and accidentally scratched herself with one of them, a grazing which as you know can have only one result. Before the wound could heal, Aphrodite met Adonis—a young man so handsome that even today we call a man of exceptional attractiveness an "Adonis"—and immediately fell deeply in love with him. The only joy of the goddess was to be with him, her only purpose to go with him wherever he went. Adonis loved hunting above all things, so he and Aphrodite daily roamed the woods hunting together. Alas, another goddess also cared for Adonis. That would be Arthemis, goddess of the moon, who also enjoyed hunting. And who was jealous that Aphrodite had the beauteous lad all to himself. One day, therefore, when Aphrodite was obliged to tend to some important business on Mount Olympus, where dwelt the gods and goddesses, Arthemis sent a wild boar in the woods to kill Adonis. Long and bitterly did Aphrodite mourn for him, and it is said that she sprinkled his blood with nectar from which sprang the beautiful short-lived flower the anemone.

ADMETUS AND ALCESTIS

God Zeus once punished his son Apollo by compelling him to serve on earth as a mortal. His master would be King Admetus, who put him in charge of all the sheep of his meadows. So honorably and kindly was Apollo treated by the king that the god sought to aid him in all things. For example, Admetus wished to have as his bride the beautiful Alcestis; Apollo helped make it happen. After several years of happiness, however, Admetus became seriously ill, and it was evident that he must soon die. Anxious to repay the king, Apollo appealed to Zeus for help. The lord of heaven gave it some thought. "Well, if there be any one willing to die in the place of Admetus, his life will be taken instead of the king's." Apollo rushed back to the palace to find the king's family and friends at his bedside, in tears. Apollo explained the terms of the Zeus-sanctioned exchange that would permit their king to live. But it was a hard sell. Apollo pleaded with them, using all his powers. But they were deaf to his pleading. All but one. "I will gladly die for my husband!" cried Alcestis. Apollo was horrified. "What! You would give your young life for his? Think too of your children. Better that Admetus should die than you." But Alcestis persisted, and with sorrow Apollo accepted. Reclining on a couch, her life began to slip away even as her husband leapt up from his bed as vital and vigorous as he had ever been. It was at just this time that the great Hercules, being in the neighborhood, happened to drop by the palace. When he overheard Alcestis's agreement overcame with pity, he cried, "Never shall Death take this noble soul!" and so saying leapt forward to take on Death itself. After a long and mighty struggle, he managed to wrest Alcestis from the usually unyielding grip of Death and restore her to life and to her husband, with whom she would live happily for many more years to come. Many lovers of mythology say that this story is the most beautiful one. I cannot disagree.

PYGMALION AND GALATEA

Pygmalion was a wise king and an excellent sculptor. But he was distrustful of women, so decided to remain unmarried forever. The closest thing he had to a companion was a statue of a girl he made that became more and more beautiful and delightful as he progressed with it. He named it Galatea. One morning, he awoke to the realization that he had fallen in love with his creation. So the next time the festival of Aphrodite was celebrated in his kingdom, he went to her altar and begged the goddess that his statue be brought to life. Aphrodite listened to his prayer and told him that his wish would be granted. That night, as he hesitantly touched the hand of Galatea, the fingers of her once immobile grabbed his hand. "Galatea!" Pygmalion cried. And with a smile she moved smilingly to his embrace. Aphrodite blessed the wedding of the happy couple.

The play "My Fair Lady" is a variation of this Greek mythological story. Do not be surprised when you discover that these wonderful tales of mythology have inspired many different authors.

DAEDALUS AND ICARUS

King Minos was the ruler of the island of Crete. One of his servants, Daedalus, was the ingenious inventor who had crafted the winding, complicated tunnels of the giant Labyrinth in which lived a monster called the Minotaur. It came to pass that Daedalus lost the favor of the king, who imprisoned both him and his son Icarus. Dedalus set his mind on finding the way to escape, and eventually was able to make a pair of wings for himself and another pair for Icarus, using feathers from birds on the island that he fastened together with wax. With these wings they flew away from the island and drew toward the mainland. But Icarus was so excited by the power of flight that the wings gave him that, ignoring the warnings of his father, he flew higher and ever higher, and closer and closer to the sun, finally so high and so close that the heat of the sun melted the wax of the wings, and off dropped the feathers. The heedless young man plunged into the sea and was drowned.

The sea into which he had fallen would come to be known as the Icarian Sea. Daedalus escaped without harm.

Perhaps you will say that you have heard this story, but to read a good story is always worth repeating.

Although many Greek myths end happily, many others relate terrible tragedies. The following three stories are about unhappy people, but many great artists liked them and used them as models for their work. I hope you like them too.

HERO AND LEANDER

A young man named Leander lived on an island, and across the sea was the town of Sestos, home of a beautiful priestess named Hero. When Leander came to Sestos to honor Goddess Aphrodite, the young man and young woman fell in love at first sight. But Hero's parents disapproved of their relationship and forbad the young lovers from seeing each other. They found a way, however. Every night, Hero hung a big lantern in the tower in which she resided, and its light guided him as he swam the dividing water to join her. But one night a great storm arose. The winds blew out the lamp as the waves tossed Leander about. At last, having lost both his strength and his guided light, he perished. The next morning, the waves washed his body ashore at the very feet of Hero. Seeing her lover's body, Hero, in deep grief, threw herself from the tower into the ocean to join him in death.

Oh, these parents! What can we say? They will never understand the kids, will they? I know one thing: my grand-daughters (like their grandfather) are too good swimmers to ever drown.

PYRAMUS AND THISBE

Pyramus and Thisbe were young lovers—and neighbors—whose parents objected to their marriage. All meetings between them were strictly forbidden. One day, they discovered a crack in the wall that separated their houses, and through this crack they were able to whisper sweet nothings to each other. At length, however, they could no longer endure their enforced separation. They decided to meet. Thisbe arrived at the assigned place before Pyramus but not before a lioness that was ambling about there. At the sight of it Thisbe screamed and fled, dropping her veil as she ran. Not being very hungry at the moment, the beast made no attempt to follow, plucking up the veil in her bloody jaws, and then a moment later dropped it. When Pyramus arrived shortly thereafter he found the bloodied veil but no Thisbe. "Thisbe has been slain!" he concluded. "But she does not die alone!" With these words he slew himself with his sword. When Thisbe returned and when she saw what had happened, she slew herself with the same sword. Their blood mounted trunk of a mulberry tree and stained its fruit a deep purple. So it has remained ever since in memory of unlucky lovers.

These two tragic tales may, have inspired the modern play "West Side Story" and William Shakespeare's Romeo and Juliet.

ORPHEUS AND EURYDICE

Orpheus was a son of the god Apollo. The father gave him a lyre and he learned to play so beautifully that he enchanted with his music not only people but also even the wildest beasts in the woods. Not far away lived a lovely girl, Eurydice, with whom Orpheus fell in love. Their marriage was universally approved and they lived in great happiness.

Alas, one day she was stung by a snake and died in the arms of her husband. Heartbroken, he decided to follow Eurydice to the Underworld of Pluto and try to get her back. At last he found god Pluto and his wife Persephone. Orpheus bowed before them and played his lyre. When his music had brought tears to their eyes, he begged them to return his wife to him. Pluto could not resist and he granted the prayer of Orpheus but under one condition. "As you leave the Underworld, she will follow you," he said. "But do not look behind you until you have both left this realm entirely. If you violate this requirement, Eurydice will again be snatched from you, lost to you forever, and it won't matter what kind of tune you play." The happy pair set out on their journey back to the land of the living, Orpheus taking the lead and being careful to stare straight ahead. When the perilous journey was almost over, however, anxiety overcame Orpheus that Eurydice might have fallen. So he permitted himself a quick backward glance. There she was safe enough, but even as he glazed, she disappeared into the dark.

As we have said, myths are not beautiful because they are real but they are beautiful because they are *not* real.

THREE SHORT STORIES FROM GREEK MYTHOLOGY

Leta was a Goddess and mother of twins, girl and boy. Girl's name was Diana, boy's Apollo. When twins were little, their mother used to take them for a walk. One day they went to a pond. It was a nice warm summer day and all three of them got thirsty. Leta knew that a pond is not far where they could get water. When they arrived to the pond, a group of peasants refused to allow them to drink water by stirring the mud at the bottom of the pond. Leta pointed to the children and remanded them to be nice. But they would not allow them to come near to the pond. Then at last Leta lost her patience and remembered that she was a Goddess. She pointed her hand in anger and cried: "Never leave the pond! Let it be your place forever!" Their hands and bodies turned green and slowly they transformed into the frogs.

Arachne was the greatest weaver. She made many beautiful tapestries and people liked her work. Arachne was very proud of her skills and one day said that she could do even better tapestry than a Goddess. Athena, Goddess heard that and set a contest between two of them. It was obvious that Arachne was a spectacular weaver but unfortunately her tapestry showed pictures what Gods have ever done wrong to people. When Athena saw it she was mad on Arachne and turned her into a spider saying: "Live on, weave on".

Aurora was Greek Goddess of dawn. Every morning she flies across the sky. She loved a prince of Troy and wanted him to be forever with her. But there was a little problem, her Prince was not a God, he was mortal, and with time would get older and finally die. Aurora asks Zeus (you remember he was the main God) for help to let Prince live forever. Zeus granted her wish, but she forgot to ask Zeus to keep Prince also young forever. As she asked Zeus, Prince became forever old. One day disappointed Aurora turned her Prince into a grasshopper.

I like these 3 stories and hope you like them too. These stories like many other mythology stories are over 2,000 year old. Greek grandmothers and grandfathers made these magnificent stories for their grandchildren about the things in nature that could not explain.

Today we know more about the nature. We know that frogs are amphibians which life starts in the water from eggs those later hatches into a tadpole, and they are not nasty people around the pond. We also know that spiders and grasshoppers are arthropods with 6 or 8 legs and that they grew from eggs, and that they are not unfortunate girl and Prince.

One question:
Take spider and insect (grasshopper). Which one has 6 and which one 8 legs?

For now I will stop writing stories because you will be busy in the school and have other things to read.

Soon we will have time for more.

And do not forget, one day, we will need to tell all these stories to your little brother.

THE BIRDS IN MYTHOLOGY

Here are three stories from mythology about birds. One story is from Indian mythology, the other from Nordic mythology, and the last one from Greek mythology.

The first story is from India. In India, people liked stories about bird called **Geruda**. This bird was a symbol of power. The Indian God Vishnu used him to travel through the air.

Maybe one day you will be able to talk to your aunt Tanya about this bird, because her family is from this part of the world. Geruda was a big bird with big red wings that were 40 miles long. His body was gold, and his face was white with an eagle's beak. Geruda was an enemy of snakes, on whom he prayed at any opportunity. Geruda had a cobra for his belt, serpents on both wrists, a snake for a necklace, two snakes as earrings, and one snake in his hair. Isn't this similar to Medusa from Greek mythology—the monster that had snakes on her head instead of hair, and dangerous eyes? Geruda had an enemy, a giant serpent called Naga. Geruda once caught Naga by seizing it by its head. But Naga learned that by swallowing large stones, Naga could make itself too heavy to carry. A magician told Geruda how to grab Naga by the tail and force it to vomit up the stones. There are many other mythological stories about this bird from countries neighboring India, such as Burma, Indonesia, and Nepal. Here you can see a picture of Geruda. There are many more, and in all of them, Geruda looks impressive.

The second story is about birds in Norse mythology. There were two ravens called **Hugin** (Mind) and **Munin** (Memory) who were companions of Odin, the chief God in Norse mythology. Odin had a large empire, and many enemies, so he needed very good police. These two birds had a mission to fly around the world and report what they saw to their master. The two ravens would sit on his shoulders and bring to his ears all the news they heard and saw. Odin would send them out at daybreak to fly over the whole empire, and they would come back at breakfast time to tell him what was going on. Forever after, ravens were thought of as spies, and people were afraid to speak in front of them.

The third story is from Greek mythology. It is about **Phoenix**, the bird of fire. One day in the beginning times, the sun looked down and saw a large bird with shimmering feathers. They were red, bright gold, and dazzling like the sun itself. The Sun called out, "Glorious Phoenix, you will be my bird and live forever. Live forever!" Phoenix was overjoyed to hear these words. He lifted his head and sang, "Sun, glorious sun, I shall sing my songs for you forever." But Phoenix was not happy for long. Poor bird. His feathers were far too beautiful. Men, women and children were always chasing him and trying to trap him. They wanted to have some of those beautiful, shiny feathers for themselves. "I cannot leave here," Phoenix said, and flew away. Phoenix flew for a long time, and came to a hidden desert where no humans lived. Here in the desert, Phoenix lived in peace, flying freely and singing his songs. Almost five hundred years passed. Phoenix was still alive, but he had grown old. He was often tired and had lost much of his strength. "I do not want to live like this," thought Phoenix. "I want to be young and strong." So Phoenix lifted his head and sang, "Sun, glorious sun, make me young and strong again," but Sun did not answer. Day after day, Phoenix sang. When the sun still did not answer, Phoenix decided to return to the place where he had lived before. Phoenix flew across the desert, and when at last he came to the place that had once been his home, Phoenix built a nest. Now everything was ready, and Phoenix sang, "Sun, glorious sun, make me young and strong again." This time, Sun heard the song and from the sky shone down with all its power. The animals, snakes, lizards, and every other bird hid from the sun's fierce rays. Only Phoenix sat on his nest and let Sun's rays beat down on his beautiful, shiny feathers. Suddenly there was a flash of light, flames leaped out of the nest, and Phoenix became a big round blaze of fire. After a while, the flames died down. The tree was not burned, nor was the nest. But Phoenix was gone. In the nest was only a heap of gray ash. The ash began to tremble, and slowly, under the ash, there rose up a young Phoenix. Young Phoenix lifted his head and sang, "Sun, glorious sun, I shall sing my songs for you forever!" "Now," said Phoenix, "I must go back to the faraway desert." Phoenix lives there still. But every five hundred years, when he begins to feel weak and old, he flies to Sun. The Sun burns him to ashes, but each time, a young Phoenix rises up.

This is a nice story, like many other stories of Greek mythology. I hope you like it. There is something interesting about Phoenix. You have heard about the state of Arizona and its capital, Phoenix. About 150 years ago, one of the first settlers in Arizona named a small place in the desert Phoenix. This small place that slowly grew from a dry, hot patch of desert and sand to the capital of Arizona and the home of the Arizona Cardinals, Arizona Diamondbacks, and Arizona Suns, reminded this settler of a bird that rose from the ashes.

THE CONSTELLATIONS OF THE NORTHERN STARS

(The Mythology Story of Cassiopeia and Andromeda)

These constellations of stars include Cassiopeia, Andromeda, Cepheus, Perseus, and Pegasus. These constellations are named after characters from a story in Greek mythology. I do not remember if we have talked about this story yet. I made a picture of the Northern constellations of the stars so that you could see how the ancient Greeks placed the characters of the story next to each other. There is also a picture of a wall painting from Pompeii that shows one segment of the drama. Pompeii was a town that was buried in lava from the volcano Vesuvius many years ago. After centuries, people in Italy cleaned the ashes and discovered exceptional examples of the Roman culture and art.

Here is the story.

Andromeda was the daughter of the Egyptian king Cepheus and his wife Cassiopeia. Her mother, Cassiopeia, claimed with foolish pride that her daughter was more beautiful than the daughters of Poseidon (the Romans called him Neptune), the god of the sea. To say something like that against the gods was an inexcusable sin. To punish the queen for her arrogance, the angry Poseidon sent a sea monster to ravage the coast of Egypt, including the kingdom of the vain queen. The desperate king consulted an Oracle, who said that no respite would be found until he sacrificed his daughter Andromeda. To save the country, Andromeda's parents ordered Andromeda to be chained to a cliff on the coast as a sacrifice to the sea monster. Our hero from a previous story, the young Greek warrior Perseus, was returning from having slain Medusa. Flying over Egypt on his winged white stallion, he happened to see the chained beauty. Before the sea monster could reach her, Perseus killed it and set Andromeda free. At that moment, they fall in love. After getting married, they went to his native island, where they had seven sons and two daughters.

This mythological story has a happy ending. Many of them do not, but we love all of them because they are so beautiful.

I want to say a few more words about the wall painting from the city of Pompeii. You can see Andromeda chained to a sea cliff on it, the body of the sea monster killed by Perseus at the lower left. In his left hand, Perseus still holds Medusa's head. This story inspired many artists in later centuries, including the famous painters Rubens and Rembrandt as well as sculptors. I did not want to make copies of the art done by later painters because it typically shows Andromeda hanging naked on the cliff. Your parents would not approve of those pictures, but many artists believed that, in order to show human beauty, the model needed to be naked.

On the page showing the star constellations, you can see that Andromeda's mother Cassiopeia was placed in the sky bound to a chair that keeps sinking and appearing near the cold Polaris as a punishment after enraging the gods. Her husband, Cepheus, is next to her. To complete the legend, Perseus, Andromeda, and Pegasus are found in the sky near the king and queen.

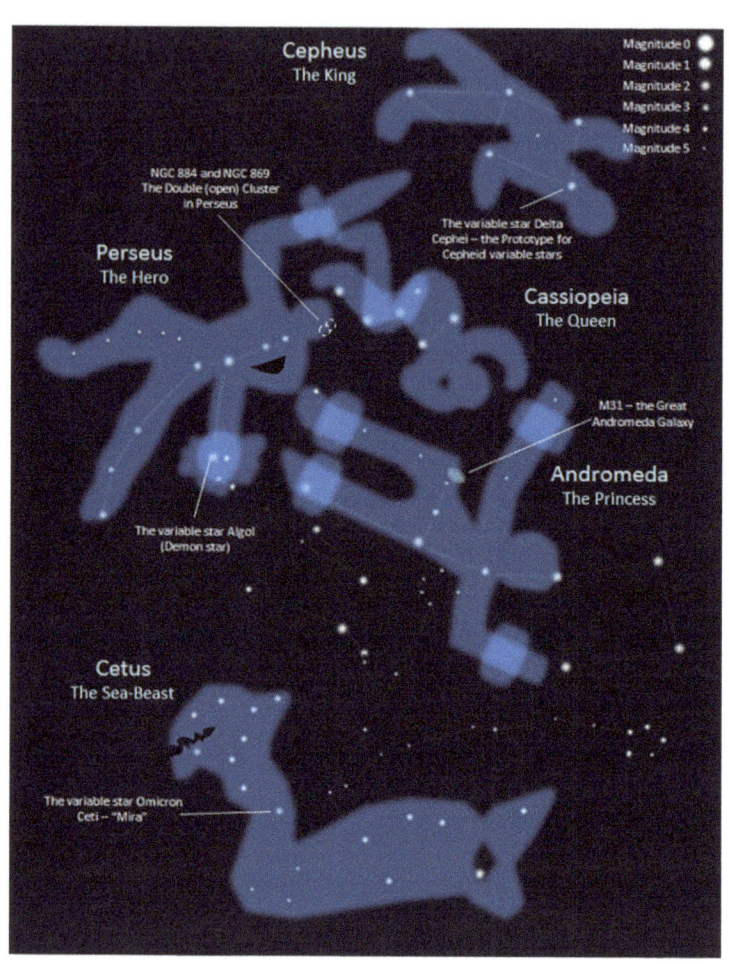

Cepheus
The King

Magnitude 0
Magnitude 1
Magnitude 2
Magnitude 3
Magnitude 4
Magnitude 5

NGC 884 and NGC 869
The Double (open) Cluster
in Perseus

The variable star Delta
Cephei – the Prototype for
Cepheid variable stars

Perseus
The Hero

Cassiopeia
The Queen

M31 – the Great
Andromeda Galaxy

Andromeda
The Princess

The variable star Algol
(Demon star)

Cetus
The Sea-Beast

The variable star Omicron
Ceti – "Mira"

THE HALLOWEEN
ANIMALS

Today, I will tell you about two little animals that people like to use as costumes for Halloween. Maybe you can guess what I will talk about. I'm going to talk about bats and spiders. Why do people like to imitate bats or spiders and be Batman and Spider-Man? It is because these two little animals are very special and also very different!

Let's talk first about bats. The bat is the only mammal that is capable of flying. It has no real wings like a bird; instead, as all mammals do, the bat has hands – just with very long fingers. Its hands look like the wings of birds because between it has webs between its fingers. I attached a picture of its hands that you can see.

The bat is a very important animal for people because bats eat insects. A single bat can eat up to 1000 mosquitoes in one hour. Without them, we would have mosquitoes all over the place. Bats also hunt rats, birds, lizards, and frogs. In South America, there is even a blood-sucking vampire bat, which people also like to imitate on Halloween. How bats hunt is very interesting. Although they cannot see well, they hunt at night using their excellent hearing. Bats can make sounds that bounce off of objects, sending echoes. From these echoes, the bats learn the size of the objects, how far away they are, and how they are traveling, all in a split second. Isn't this fascinating? Talking about echoes, I would like to remind you about a girl called Echo from

Greek mythology. She returned the same words back to people all of the time, such as, "Who are you?" or "What is your name?" Bats at rest hang with their heads facing down!!!!! They grasp whatever they're hanging from with their clawed feet. When they detect their prey with their echo system, they take off into flight from this position. Why do people like to dress as Batman on Halloween? Maybe it's because they want to be superheroes like Batman, who helps many people and children that are in trouble. Or maybe they would like to be able to fly using a bat's echo system. I am sure that you could find some other reasons.

The other story that I want to tell is about another little animal – the spider. On Halloween, people like to dress up like Spider-Man, another superhero who helps people in trouble. There are many stories about spiders. You already know one of them, although I might need to remind you a little bit. This is another story from Greek mythology. It is about a girl called Arachne who was an excellent weaver and who challenged the goddess in weaving. At the end of the competition, the goddess lost and got very angry, so she changed the girl into a spider. Because of this, our name for spiders and their family is Arachnids. There is another story about spiders that I would like to tell you. This story comes from Germany. If you have ever looked at the beautiful tinsel sparkling on your Christmas tree and wondered who came up with the idea of decorating the tree this way, wonder no longer. According to German legend, it was a Christmas miracle. On Christmas Eve, when night came and all of the people were at home in bed, the spiders snuck into the room. To their amusement, in the middle of the living room was a beautifully decorated Christmas tree. They were so excited that they ran all over the tree. A gray web now covered the whole tree. When Santa arrived with presents, he was amused to see the tree covered in spider webs. Now, he was faced with a dilemma.

He did not want to disappoint the family by letting them see their beautiful tree covered with spider webs. However, the spiders were so pleased with their work that he did not have the heart to take it down. What could he do? He thought and thought and came up with a wonderful idea. He turned all of the webs into beautiful shiny silver stands. When the family came into the room in the morning, they saw their tree sparkling and glittering in the morning sun. Their delight was unsurpassed. They had never seen such a beautiful tree. From that day on, tinsel become a treasured ornament for Christmas trees all over the world. Those who know the legend make sure that they give thanks to the hard-working spiders by hanging beautiful ornaments on their trees. But why do people dress like spiders on Halloween? Maybe it's because Spider-Man helps the police to catch bad guys with his webs, similar to spiders that catch bad insects in their webs.

Remember:

Spiders have four pairs of legs, while insects have three.

The bat is the only mammal that can fly.

And it is so nice that we meet characters from Greek mythology like Echo and Arachne so often in our stories.

When I get you in my webs, there will be a lot of dunking!!!!!!

This is the end of my collection of mythology stories made for you.

The following pages are about different topics most of them not heard in the school.

CALENDAR

Let's talk today about the calendar and its months. You may think that this will be boring, but I would like to tell you that it is not. You have already heard about the Romans and their empire. These are the people who invented the calendar that we still use today. To understand the names of the months that the Romans chose, however, we need some explanation. For example, the names for months of September, October, November, and December come from the Latin words Septem, Octo, Novem and Decem. In Latin, "Septem" means seven, "Octo" means eight, "Novem" means nine, and "Decem" means ten. Everything sounds fine, but there is something that does not fit! Actually, we count these months differently. September is not the seventh month in our calendar, and October, November, and December are not eighth, ninth, and tenth months in our calendar.

Why is that? Who would make a calendar like that?

The Romans made this calendar over 2000 years ago. Did they make a big mistake? No, the Romans did not make a mistake. They knew how to count the months.

So: here starts our story. The Romans were military people, warriors and solders. They were always fighting in wars to get more land and goods. They occupied many countries, but they never had enough. In winter, they did not go to war. Instead, they went home to be with their families and friends and have a rest. For them, it was not important to count this time of the year. They only started to count the days once winter was over and the weather became nicer, so they could start military training and planning for new wars. When the weather became warmer, they named the first month by their god of war – Mars. Today, we call this month March. As you can see, the Romans did not have January and February. They started their calendar with March. After March, they named the months after different gods, goddesses, or important people. The second month was April, which gets its name from the Latin word for "to open," reminding the Romans that this is the time of year when the flowers open on the trees.

May – Maia was a Greek goddess of fertility.

June – The goddess Juno was the Roman goddess of marriage. The most marriages happen in June.

July – This was named in honor of the great emperor Julius Caesar.

August – This month got its name in honor of Emperor Augustus.

For the last four months, the Romans used the numbers 7, 8, 9, and 10. You can see that their calendar, 2000 years ago, only had 10 months. They used that calendar for a long time. Many years later, the Romans changed it to a 12-month calendar.

Why did they do that? Again, the reason was their military and their wars. In Rome, at the beginning of the year, new governors were selected for their colonies. Governors were very important people because they kept the colonies in order and under control. So every year on March 1, a new group of governors were selected for the colonies. It was like that until the year 156 BC, when a revolution started in the Roman colony of Hispania just before March 1 and the selection of a new governor. The old governor had already left Hispania, and the new one had not arrived yet to give the orders. Because of this, the Romans lost a lot of land. To avoid such a problem in the future, the Romans decided to start the selection of governors earlier and added two months to the year, January and February. This way, the selection of new governors started earlier, and the Roman calendar got 12 months. This is the same calendar that we use today.

Now, they needed names for the new months. The first month, January, was named after Janus, their god of doorways! This god had two faces looking in opposite directions to see the past and the future. In other words, he was looking at the old and the new year.

February comes from the Latin word for purification, which means cleaning. This is the month of Lent and Ash Wednesday and the time of the year when we go to church to get cleansed of our sins. Now, we have a complete 12-month calendar.

In the time of the Roman Empire, Nick and Luka would have had birthdays in the seventh instead of the ninth month of the year, and Lauren and Lia would have had theirs in the ninth, not the eleventh month every year. One important month for you to remember is October. Maybe you know why. This is the month when your both grandmothers and Didi have their birthdays. Today, you read about something that many people have not had the chance to learn, and it should not have been boring.

THE GREAT WARRIORS

A long time before Christopher Columbus came to America, only Indian tribes lived on this continent. They lived a nomadic life, occasionally battling over land, food, and horses.

However, across the ocean in Europe, life was much more complicated and dangerous. Many big empires fought long and brutal wars there with heavy losses of people's lives. In these wars, there were people who distinguished themselves as leaders and became so famous that many books were written about them and their wars and victories.

Here is a brief article about five warriors that played an important role in the history of mankind. All of them were famous and popular during their lives. They lived at different times, but all of them had a common wish – to win and conquer. It sounds funny, but yet another common characteristic between at least four of these five men was shortness of stature. A question that is often asked is: Are short people more rebellious and inclined to battle? I think that there may be some truth in this.

In this account, we will start with ancient Greece and their hero.

ALEXANDER THE GREAT
(356-323 BC)

Why "the Great"? Even today, we think that he was the greatest military commander of all time. He never lost a battle!Alexander the Great lived 2000 years ago. He was a king's son. His father was the king of Macedon (a small state in Europe, north of Greece). One day, when Alexander was 13, he went with his father to a market to buy a black stallion. However, there was no one to tame the horse. The father lost interest in buying it, but Alexander did not. He promised to pay for the horse himself if he should fail to tame it. Alexander noticed that the horse was afraid of its shadow, so he spoke softly to it and turned it toward the sun so that it could not see its own shadow. He then jumped on it and successfully tamed the horse. This horse later carried him into all of his battles. Alexander named it Bucephales, meaning ox-head. Bucephales carried him as far as India; when the horse died due to old age, Alexander named a city after it.

Alexander's father sent his son to a very good school. In the school, Alexander had the best teachers and met many boys his own age. Some of them became his good friends. When Alexander became king, he made these classmates the generals of his army. Wasn't that nice?

When Alexander was 20, his father was assassinated at the wedding of his daughter. Thereafter, Alexander became the king. Soon, he started his military campaign. He was very short, but was a very brave and strong warrior.

From Macedon, he went with his army to conquer Greece, Turkey, Syria, Egypt, and then back into the north to Afghanistan, Pakistan, and finally, India. One after the other, these countries became parts of his empire where he spread Greek culture. He even built cities and gave them his name – Alexandria. At the end of his campaign, there were about 20 cities named Alexandria. The most famous one is still in Egypt, where Alexander was buried in a golden coffin.

There is an anecdote about Alexander the Great. When he was in Turkey, he visited the city of Gordian. In this city, there was a big knot, which to that date nobody could untie. It was said that whoever untied the Gordian knot would one day rule the entire world.

When Alexander heard that, he went to untie it. He tried a few times with no luck. He did not give up; instead, he simply slashed the knot with his sword. This was not exactly what he was supposed to do, but he did untie it. Today, when we need to do something that looks impossible, we say, "This is Gordian knot." You will hear people saying that. Alexander was the greatest warrior of all time. He died of malaria at a relatively young age, and his Empire was left to his good generals.

Alexander never lost a battle, despite typically being outnumbered. He was a winner due to the Greek phalanx, a good cavalry, his bold strategy, and the fierce loyalty of his troops. The phalanx is a formation of solders that are armed with spears 20 feet long.

HANNIBAL (247–181 BC)

My dearest grandchildren, do you remember the story about the battle on the Marathon, the battle between two powerful Empires: Persia and Greece?

Here is another story about two other Empires that did not like each other. One was the Roman Empire, the other the Carthaginian Empire. The Roman Empire was in Europe, in what today is Italy. Its capital was Rome. The Carthaginian Empire was in North Africa, in the lands that today are Egypt, Libya, Tunisia, Algeria, and Morocco. It also spread into Europe, in what today is southern Spain as well as the islands of Corsica and Sicily. Its capital was Carthage in Africa, a place that does not exist anymore.

If you look at the map, you could see that these two Empires were separated by water, the Mediterranean Sea.

The Carthaginians had a very good army and cavalry, but their main strength was their African war elephants. Neither men nor horses could fight against elephants carrying warriors armed with spears and arrows.

Most importantly, they had Hannibal, an excellent general. He lived from 247 to 181 BC. His father was one of the leading commanders, and young Hannibal begged his father to take him into the battles. Hannibal's father agreed, but demanded that Hannibal swear that, as long as he lived, he would never be a friend of Rome.

Hannibal lived during a period of great tension in the Mediterranean, when the Roman Republic was trying to establish its supremacy over the other great powers of Carthage and Greece. Despite this, Hannibal decided to attack the Roman Empire. He needed to take his army from Africa over the Mediterranean Sea, but he could not do this because the Romans were a superior sea power that could easily fight off any invasion from Carthage.

Instead, he decided to take a different route and led his army and elephants across Northern Africa to Gibraltar, where they then traveled to Spain by ship. From Spain, he went with 25,000 men and 80 war elephants to Rome. On this long trip to Rome, he needed to pass over high mountains, the Pyrenees and the Alps. Unfortunately, in the winter, all but one of the elephants died. This tragedy weakened Hannibal a lot, but it did not stop him.

On the other side of the mountains, the Roman army rushed to meet Hannibal. They had 600,000 solders, many more than Hannibal's army.

The two armies met at a lake. Around the lake were hills with woods. Here, Hannibal made a plan. At night, he told his solders to go into the hills and tie torches to the horns of a herd of cattle so that they would look like an army on the move and making camps. Meanwhile, he escaped in another direction in the woods.

When the Romans saw the lights on the hills, they wanted to surprise their enemy. They thought that they just needed to go alongside the lake to the hills to do this. When they came closer to the lake, however, Hannibal rushed with his army from the woods and pushed the Romans into the water. Then, he ordered his cavalry to hit them from the front and back. This ended the fight.

That was only one of Hannibal's victories in Italy. He and his army occupied a large part of Italy and stayed there for 15 years.

After his victories in Italy, he could have easily gone on and captured the capital of the Roman Empire, Rome. "Hannibal ante portas" (Hannibal at the door) was heard in Rome from the scared people, many of whom left the city in panic.

However, Rome's occupation never happened.

Why didn't Hannibal get to the Roman capital?

While he was fighting with the Romans in Europe, Rome sent a general with an army to Hannibal's homeland in Africa. Hannibal's country needed urgent help. Because of this, our famous general stopped planning to attack Rome and went back home on his ships instead.

At home, he found new war elephants and fresh warriors who were strong and ready to defend their country. The Romans were strong too, though. They had a large army and cavalry and a good general. His name was Scipio.

Scipio knew that he needed to do something to fight efficiently against the Carthaginian war elephants. He made a plan to scare and frighten the animals with a terrible noise by having his men loudly play trumpets. The elephants were so frightened by this that they started to run into Hannibal's solders and horses. After that, Scipio had no problem winning. Hannibal was defeated.

Hannibal was 43 years old when he lost the war. He could not stay at home after that. He went into exile in Greece and later

West Asia, where he was always welcomed as a military advisor. The Romans, however, were determined to hunt him down, and when he finally fell into his enemies' hands, he took a poison that he had long carried with him in a ring.

That was the end of one of the greatest warriors in history. Hannibal is ranked by many people as one of the greatest commanders that the world has ever seen and is often placed second after Alexander the Great. His military tactics and strategies were discussed later by many famous generals and were always highly regarded.

Here, I would like to mention one of Hannibal's admirers, the Greek general Pyrrhus, who was also a distinguished warrior in his time. Pyrrhus defeated the Romans in an important war, but that was a costly victory. The Romans lost 7,000 men, while Pyrrhus lost 3,000, including many of his best generals. When people today want to say that something was successful at a high cost, they say, "This was a Pyrrhic victory."

There is something else that is important about Pyrrhus. When he returned home, he went to intervene in a civil dispute in a city. He was trapped in a narrow street while he was fighting with a solder. The solder's mother, who was watching from the roof, threw a tile that knocked Pyrrhus from his horse and broke his spine, paralyzing him. The solder then beheaded him. That was a tragic end for a great general.

This was a short deviation from our main topic of the greatest warriors in history, but I wanted you to know what a Pyrrhic victory is.

About one hundred years later, another great warrior was born, but this time not in Carthage. This warrior belonged to the Roman Republic. The story goes that he was born with the help of a surgical procedure that today bears his name – the Caesarian section.

JULIUS CAESAR (100 – 44 BC)

While Julius Caesar led their military, the Roman Republic, for the first time in history, conquered the Gauls in Central Europe and invaded Great Britain. These achievements granted Caesar an unmatched military power.

However, there were many jealous senators in Rome who wanted to limit his future power. They ordered him to disband his army and return to Rome. Caesar thought he would be prosecuted if he entered Rome, so he crossed the border, the river Rubicon, with his army. This ignited a civil war in the Roman Republic.

When crossing the river Rubicon, he said in Greek, "Alea iacta est." Let the die be cast. These famous words are worthwhile to remember and use when you do something decisive.

Soon, Caesar became the leader in Rome. During his tenure, he helped lower- and middle-class people, awarded his army with land, and became very popular. In the Senate, however, this led to angst and concerns that Caesar wanted to be a king. Rome had never had a king, instead being ruled by a Senate. To see a man change the political system was against the Senate's wish.

On March 15, the date when the Romans celebrated the New Year (you'll remember that the Romans didn't have the months of January and February in their calendar), the Senate held a meeting. Caesar attended this meeting, and 60 conspirators, led by Brutus, came to the meetinghouse with daggers concealed in their togas. They struck Caesar at least 23 times.

Legend has it that Caesar said to Brutus, who was one of his favorite students and who stubbed him last, "You, too, my child?" There is a picture showing the death of Caesar.

With the death of Caesar, Rome lost a great man who was more successful as a general than as a politician.

There are two more great warriors that I would like to talk about. Both of them were born a long time after Alexander the Great, Hannibal, and Julius Caesar. One of them was a Hun, and the other was a Mongol.

The Huns were a nomadic people who lived in the steppes of Central Asia. They started moving from their homes in the 1st century AD. The Mongolian empire was formed in the 11th century. The Huns and the Mongols were most likely related, since they lived in the same territory in Asia and had similar cultural characteristics, despite being separated by about 1000 years.

Although the Greek, Roman, and Carthaginian armies were merciless and brutal to their conquered populations, this cannot be compared to the brutality of those nomadic peoples from Asia. They were real barbarians in the full meaning of the word.

We will start with the Scourge of God.

ATTILA (406 - 453 AC)

Attila was king of the Huns. His name means "Little Father." In Europe, he was called the Scourge of God because he and his army were so brutal, leaving behind only destruction. The Hun hordes mercilessly massacred, looted, and burned occupied places across Europe and Asia.

These wild warriors lived on roots, herbs, and the half-raw flesh of animals, which they warmed by placing between their own thighs or against the backs of their horses. They were the wildest barbarians, using neither fire nor cooking.

Attila, furthermore, was illiterate. He colored his hair red and often powdered both his hair and mustache with golden powder. He was short, ugly, and smelled as bad as his fellow Huns.

Attila planned his campaigns without anyone else's help. One of his favorite tactics was to hide his troops until they were within arrow range of his target and then attack quickly, one rank firing at high angles to cause the defenders to raise the shields, another firing directly into enemy lines. The Huns were skilled archers. They could shoot arrows from horseback at full gallop, and they fought in close combat with swords. They also often threw nets over their enemies.

Attila had 12 wives. He died on his wedding night with the 12th wife, drunk and choking on the blood from his own nosebleed.

Attila invaded Europe and was a big danger to the Roman Empire. When he came close to Rome, the Roman negotiators offered him gold and jewelry. This made Attila happy, and he decided to return back to the north.

From Asia came another man who conquered more land than anyone else. He was brutal and dangerous like Attila, but he was good for his country, trying to modernize it and open it to foreign cultures. Today, he is a celebrated person in Mongolia.

GENGHIS KHAN (1162-1227)

Genghis Khan was born on the border of Mongolia and Siberia. Legend has it that he came to the world clutching a blood clot in his right hand. His name translates to "Universal Ruler."

At this time, dozens of nomadic tribes in the central Asian steppes were constantly fighting and stealing from each other. Genghis Khan united these tribes and put competent allies rather than family members into key positions. To suppress wars, he abolished aristocratic titles, forbade selling and kidnapping women, punished livestock thefts with death, allowed freedom of religion, introduced writing, and welcomed diplomats from other countries. He (and later, his successors) greatly modernized Mongolian culture. You may remember that Marco Polo visited Mongolia and stayed as a welcome guest and adviser to the government for many years.

Genghis Khan's first military campaign outside of Mongolia was against kingdom of China. After several wars against China, he turned west and conquered more than twice as much land as any other person in history. His empire extended from Japan to the Caspian Sea.

Similarly to the Huns, his army consisted almost entirely of cavalrymen who were expert riders and deadly with bows and arrows. I copied two pictures that show the Mongols in action. One of Genghis Khan's signature tactics was to have a false withdrawal, then ambush the enemy. He was also very successful in siege warfare by cutting his target's supplies of food and taking prisoners and forcing them to return to the sieged cities, causing shortages of food and starvation.

He died after injuries sustained from falling off of a horse. He did not like pictures to be drawn of him, so we do not know if he was short in stature like the other great warriors. The art pictures show Mongol's in the attack.

And at the end of these stories, we can say that maybe our good Indian tribes and their buffalo should have been happy that they were far away from these people on another continent. However, unfortunately for them, that was not the case for too long.

MARCO POLO

This story is about the explorers. You already have heard about Christopher Columbus and Ferdinand Magellan, but there were many more at that time. We will talk about some of them today. One might ask, why they were doing that? Why they were taking long and dangerous trips? Did they want to find new continents, islands, interesting places—or it was something else? All these famous navigators wanted to find one thing: expensive goods that would make them rich and famous. They wanted to find gold, silver, jewelry, spices, silk, and things like that. They knew that these places were in India and China, but to get there, one needed to travel by land on the so-called "Silk Road." The Silk Road started in Europe and went through Asia to China and India.

Marco Polo was one traveler who went to China and Mongolia by the Silk Road. He came back home to Italy very rich and famous. Marco may have been born in Croatia. That was nine hundred years ago, so it is difficult to know if this is true or not. His father and uncle were good traders with gold and jewelry. They went to China to trade, and on one such trip, they took young Marco, who was twenty years old. Their travel was long but safe. At that time, the Silk Road was under the Mongolian Empire, and the Mongolian Khan (this is what they called their king) liked travelers and traders from Europe, so he protected their trips. The worst part of the Silk Road was the route through the Gobi Desert. Marco Polo wrote in his book after returning home that the Gobi Desert is so long that it takes a year to go from one end to the other, and it takes one month to cross it from one side to the other at the narrowest place. He said that the Gobi Desert was only sand, with nothing to eat or drink.

When Marco came to the Mongolian Empire, he was welcomed by the Khan, who later became his good friend. The Khan liked Marco and wanted to hear about Europe and its people. Marco stayed in Mongolia for seventeen years, learning the language and seeing many interesting things. One thing that fascinated him was the system of mail. The mail and messages were delivered by men. There was important and less important mail. Important mail was carried by a horseman, who went twenty-five miles to a station where another fresh horse was waiting, letting him continue to the next station, and so on. This mail could travel in one day for two hundred and fifty to three hundred miles. The less important mail was carried by foot-runners. They had stations three miles apart and carried a belt with bells to alert people that mail was arriving. Marco became very rich in Mongolia, and after seventeen years, he decided to go back to his country of Italy. But there was one big problem. In those seventeen years, the Silk Road had become very dangerous and difficult. It was dangerous because there were many bandits waiting for the caravans with gold and jewelry, and difficult because the Silk Road went through Turkey, where travelers needed to pay high road taxes. Marco was intelligent and resourceful; he decided to go home by the sea. He would travel from China to the South China Sea, around Sumatra to the Indian Ocean and Persian Gulf, and then by land to the Black Sea. His good friend the Khan gave him a golden tablet and an order to have food and supplies brought to him when he traveled on the land. The Khan also gave him two thousand horsemen to escort him through dangerous places. After Marco came to Constantinople, he sailed to Venice, Italy.

Two hundred years later, the Silk Road was not popular anymore. This is why the famous navigators were planning different ways to go to India and China. There were many brave men who did this, mainly from Portugal, Spain, and Italy. The first one who tried to sail east was from Portugal. His name was Bartholomew Dias. His plan was to get to India by going around Africa. He did not get further than the Cape of Good Hope, however, because his crew was afraid to continue. He turned back and went home. He is the one who called the southernmost point of Africa the Cape of Good Hope, in the hope that someone would one day find India by traveling around it. A few years later, Christopher Columbus had a different plan. He decided to travel from Spain across the Atlantic Ocean because he believed that there was no land between Europe and Asia. He was surprised to find only primitive people and no gold in the New World. The next navigator from Europe was another one from Portugal. His name was Vasco da Gama. He sailed around Africa and was luckier than Dias. He arrived in India and found what he was looking for—gold, jewelry, and spices. He went home and became rich and famous.

There were many more explorers, but let's mention only one more, one who is very important. He was from Portugal, and his name was Ferdinand Magellan. He knew that the best spices were in Indonesia on the Spice Islands. Why were spices were so important? Spices are like sugar, salt, and ketchup—things that give better taste to food. At that time, spices were rare in Europe and very expensive! Magellan wanted to find as much spices as he could and bring them back to Portugal. His plan was not to go around Africa; rather, he planned to go around South America. He crossed the narrow strait that he named Magellan Strait, and sailed into a nice, peaceful ocean that he named the Pacific Ocean (the word Pacific is of Roman origin and means "peace"). After sailing on the Pacific for several months, he came to Indonesia and its islands with excellent spices but very unfriendly tribes. In fighting with them, Magellan was wounded in the head and by a poisonous arrow in the leg. A few days later, he died on the ship. His sailors continued and came safely back home.

When you will have a chance, look for:

Portugal

Cape of Good Hope

Gobi Desert

Mongolia

Indonesia—a group of many islands

Venice, Italy

Soon you will be coming to Florida, and we will have more time to talk about what kind of stories you like—stories from mythology, or stories about explorers, famous warriors, stars, or something else. I would like you to hear as much as you can and remember them all, so that one day you can tell them to Theo. One day when you, Nick, and you, Luka, will read to him, I am sure that Theo will appreciate it.

THE EXPEDITION
TO THE
SOUTH POLE

This story starts in Norway, a country that is not difficult for you to find on the map of Europe.

In Norway, there was a man named Amundsen who liked to go to new places. One day, he decided to be the first to reach the South Pole. Norway is very far from the South Pole, but this was not a problem for Amundsen, and he started to make plans for a long journey.

First, he needed a good team. He looked for a doctor, a ski-maker, a cook, and a skillful dog driver. All of the members of his team needed to be excellent skiers and good cross-country runners. It was not very difficult to find such a group of men in Norway, where the winters are long and full of snow.

Amundsen also knew that it would be very important to have good skis, sledges, warm clothing, and tents. Dogs would need to pull the sledges a long way, so he bought the best sledge dogs from Greenland. In Greenland, dogs help people every day with sledges on the ice and snow and can stand cold weather very well.

What was his plan for traveling?

His plan was to sail from Norway to South America, to go around Cape Horn (look later in the atlas for this dangerous place), and then go up to San Francisco, your birthplace, to get some fresh food and water. From San Francisco, they would sail south to the Bay of Whales in Antarctica.

The journey from Norway took four months. In the Bay of Whales, they made a camp. They waited until October to start the long trip to the South Pole.

Do you have any idea why they waited for wintertime in the Southern Hemisphere to start their journey? I have asked you that before; do you still remember? Of course you do.

Amundsen left the camp with four team members, four sledges with supplies, and 52 dogs. Ooh la la, that's a lot of dogs!

It took them 99 days to find the South Pole. There, they put up a Norwegian flag, gave each other high fives, made a tent, and left a letter inside with their names on it.

On the way back, they encountered some very bad freezing weather and cold wind with snowstorms – but all of them arrived safely at the camp in the Bay of Whales. Everyone was very happy. However, there was one sad thing, which was that some of the dogs did not survive the cold, and only 11 of them came back home. If I had been there, I would have given a big present to these hero dogs, like vanilla ice cream or peppers with humus.

You may have some questions about this interesting expedition. I was not able to write everything down, but we will have a chance to talk about them one day.

Wait, this is not the end.

At the same time that Amundsen was planning his expedition, there was a man in England who wanted to do the same and be the first to reach the South Pole. His name was Scott. He was a navy officer who spent most of his life on ships and the sea.

Scott had a team that had little training on the ice and snow. Although he purchased skis and dogs, he was not convinced that they were the key to his trip's success.

Scott believed that manpower without the help of animals would be good enough for the journey to the South Pole. He also believed that ponies would do better than dogs and sent a member of his team to Manchuria to buy ponies and to Siberia to buy dogs. Siberia and Manchuria are places in Asia that have very long and cold winters. Scott knew nothing about horses and thought that he would not much need them.

What was his plan?

His plan was to sail from England to Cape Horn and go around New Zealand to his final destination, McMurdo Sound in Antarctica. There, he would make camp and start the final preparations with sledges that would be pulled by ponies, dogs, and men.

Scott and his team left the camp at the same time as Amundsen left his camp. On the way through the snow and cold, though, all of Scott's ponies and dogs died. Now, the men needed to pull the sledges by themselves. This was very difficult, but they did reach the South Pole, although it was five weeks later than Amundsen.

It was a big disappointment for them to see the Norwegian flag on the South Pole and to find the tent with Amundsen's letter in it.

On the long way back to camp, Scott and his team needed to pull the sledges with their food and supplies throughout freezing winds, snow, and often very heavy fog. Unfortunately, they could not make it to the camp. Several months later, their friends found them on the ice, covered with snow.

This is a very sad ending.

Scott was a brave person who overestimated the power of man. He believed that men could overpower nature with just a little help from animals.

Let me tell you one thing – it is good to be brave like Scott, but it is better to be brave and smart, like Amundsen.

Maybe you have already found:

The Bay of Whales

McMurdo Sound

Cape Horn

San Francisco

New Zealand

Siberia

Manchuria

Now go, my dear grandchild, and sleep if you are in bed and dream about skiing with sledge dogs.

Laku noc (Croatian for Good night).

THE EXPEDITION
TO THE
NORTH POLE

L et me tell you first about The North Pole, and then we will talk about the expeditions to it.

North Pole is in the middle of Arctic Ocean. You cannot get there by the water because this part of the Arctic Ocean is covered with ice sea. This is a large ice cap, which is floating in the ocean and shifting all the time. The sea depth at the North Pole is about 13,000 feet, this equals to the length of 100 soccer fields!

Now we see that North Pole is very much different than South Pole. The South Pole is not a floating ice in the ocean, it is rather a land covered with ice and snow.

After this short introduction about the North Pole let's talk about expeditions to this place.

There were many people from different countries who tried to find North Pole. Some were from the countries close to North Pole such as Canada, Norway, Sweden, England and USA, but other explorers came from countries, which were far from North Pole, such as Italy and Japan.

All of them tried to reach North Pole, however using different means, for example, by ship, on the skies, by plane or balloons, helicopters or snowmobiles. One man from Japan came to North Pole on the motorcycle. Most recently some people did parachute jumps from the plane to the North Pole.

A lot of fanny things happened on the North Pole.

Since in summer ice becomes thinner the submarines can surface on the North Pole. I have a picture for you showing US submarine surfaced through the ice on the North Pole.

But who came first on the North Pole?

His name is Robert Peary. He was a navy engineer. Similar to Amundsen, he had a good group of people of different specialties. Peary selected a doctor, a cook and good skiers for his travel to North Pole. The group had 25 men and some Eskimos. Peary knew that these people could help a lot.

From North America Peary sailed north to Ellesmere Island, which is north of Greenland. This is a land of Eskimo people. Here he stayed a little longer and wanted to learn from Eskimos about cold weather, winter clothing, dogs, sledges and igloo.

What is igloo?

Igloo is Eskimo's house, made of ice blocks. Eskimo eats, lives and sleeps there. Peary liked the igloos because he could use them instead of tents. The tents are heavy and large, they take a lot of space on sledges and without them he could travel much easier and faster.

Peary bought 133 Eskimo dogs and good wooden sledges.

It was a cold trip through wind, fog, and snow. It took them one month to come to North Pole. Peary with a friend and 4 Eskimos arrived to North Pole, where they left US flag and a small tent with a letter with their names.

They gave each other high 5 and turned back home. They came safely back to camp with almost all sledge-dogs.

Didi can only say: Bravo Peary, you are a good man and you took a good care of the best men's friends – dogs!

This is happy end.

We like that.

Wasn't it fanny to read about jumping with parachute and riding a motorcycle to North Pole?

Look later for?

Arctic Ocean

Canada

England

Norway

Sweden

Italy

Japan

Greenland

Ellesmere Island

So far I told you stories about the places that are far north and far south on our planet.

The next time I will write something very different, about Marathon race.

For that we will need to go back to the ancient Greece, the country from where are those beautiful mythology stories, which many of them you already know.

Now if you are in the bed go and sleep and dream about flying over the North Pole in the balloon.

And be smart - no jumping with the parachute!

Good night.

AMELIA EARHART

In 1932, Amelia Earhart flew across the Atlantic Ocean. She was the first woman who was able to do that. Her plan was to start in Newfoundland in Canada and fly to Paris, the capital of France in Europe. It took her 15 hours to fly over the Atlantic. Because of strong winds from the north and mechanical problems with the plane, she was forced to land in North Ireland rather than France. She landed in a pasture with her small plane. There were many celebrations when she came back home to America. Even President Hoover invited her to the White House to talk about the flight. The next president, President Roosevelt, was another person who was very proud of this brave woman. He even took a flight with Amelia in a small plane.

After her transatlantic flight, Amelia Earhart moved from Boston to California. There, she started to plan a longer flight. She wanted to travel around the world in a small plane with one copilot. After working for long time on the plane, she left California. On the map, you can follow her route and see the many stops where she refilled the tank and got food. Everything went fine until she came to the Pacific Ocean. She and her copilot needed two more stops before they would make it back home to California. The first stop would be on a small Pacific Island – Howland Island – and the next one would be in Hawaii. Nobody knows what happened to her over the Pacific Ocean. Amelia Earhart and her copilot disappeared over the Pacific. They never made it to Howland Island.

I am attaching the flight route so that you can see how close Amelia was to finishing her long flight. The line is her completed route, with multiple stops in North America, South America, Africa, Southern Asia, and Australia.

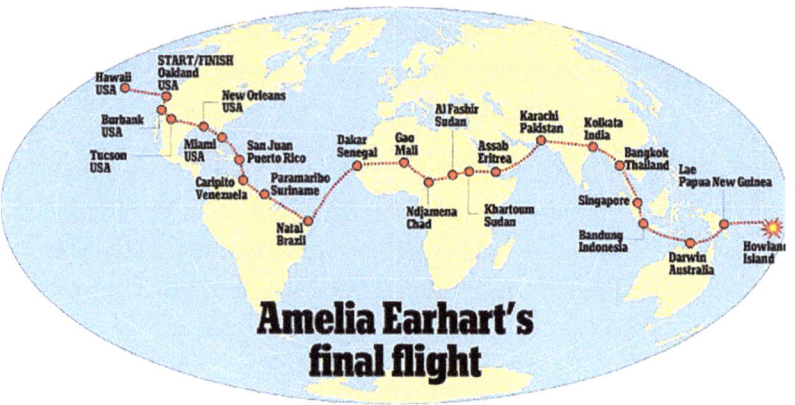

Amelia Earhart's final flight

A FAMOUS
MATHEMATICIAN

Once upon a time, there was a student in the third grade. His name was Karl Gauss. He lived in Germany, a country that many famous people like scientists, writers, musicians, painters, and sportsmen have come from. One day, his teacher gave the class a difficult test to keep them busy while he was doing something else. The test was that the teacher told the class to start adding from 1 to 100. The teacher turned around and went to his desk to start working in peace, but Gauss immediately wrote down the correct answer: 5050. The teacher could not believe it! How did Gauss do this? I do not want you to try that, since Gauss was older than you when he did the test. However, you will understand how clever he was when I tell you what he did. It is on the page below. As you can see, he made it simple. He took one number from the end and one from the front and added them to reach 101, and so on. The rest of the test was easy. At the end of the process, he had 50 x 101 = 5050.

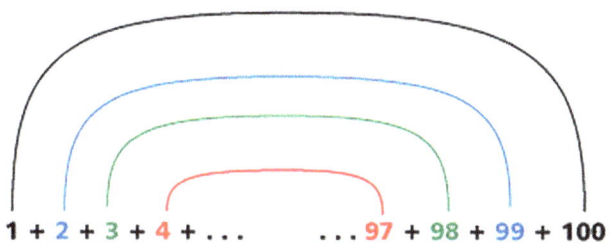

A FAMOUS PAINTER

I have another story about another famous man from Germany. His name was Albrecht Dürer, a well-known painter. When he was in art school, his teacher wanted to keep the class busy while he needed to go out. He told the class to paint the face of a man who was there as a model. Instead of doing what the teacher said, young Dürer painted a fly on the man's front. When the teacher came back to the classroom, he immediately went to the model and tried to scare off the fly. This fly looked like it was alive, Dürer was so good. One day, we will look at his paintings.

LEWIS AND CLARK

This story starts more than 200 years ago, when our President was Thomas Jefferson. For a long time, President Jefferson was planning to organize an expedition to the other side of America. He wanted to find a way to the Pacific Ocean going by rivers. Jefferson believed that there was a waterway through the Rocky Mountains and that the expedition could travel by boat the entire trip. Today, as you know, we've learned that this is not possible. At that time, though, it was a big enigma or question mark. These days, you can fly over the U.S. in six hours. Even if you have to take a car, you can do it in six days. Two hundred years ago, however, traveling from the Mississippi River to the Pacific Ocean in boats, on horseback, and on foot would take much longer. First, Jefferson hired a scientist from France to lead this expedition, but he stopped him early because he learned that this man was a French spy. After this, Jefferson looked for a man in America to be the expedition's leader. He was very happy when he found Captain Meriwether Lewis for the job. He told Lewis to take whatever he needed for the expedition and that the government would pay for it. Lewis bought a lot of supplies and gifts. He chose 44 former military men, a few professional hunters, and his good friend from the army, Sergeant William Clark, to make up his team. For the expedition, they built a special boat for sailing on the river. Before they left, Jefferson asked Lewis to take good notes of everything new that he saw on the journey. Jefferson told Lewis to make maps, collect minerals, and watch out for new animals, birds, trees, rivers, and lakes. Jefferson also told him to make friends with the Indians and give them American flags and silver coins as gifts from the President of America (the Indians called him "Big Father"). Lewis also had different tools for hunting and fishing and gifts that he was planning to exchange with the Indians for horses and canoes.

The expedition started from St. Louis when Lewis and Clark traveled on a sailing boat upstream in the Missouri River. They were able to reach North Dakota by the river, where they met a French fur trader and his wife. She was a Shoshone Indian whose name was Sacagawea. Lewis hired the fur trader and Sacagawea to go with them. Sacagawea was very helpful on this journey as an interpreter and in making friends with Indians. She went with Lewis and Clark all the way to the Pacific Ocean. On their way, they stopped many times to hunt and get food. On one such hunt, a grizzly bear started to run after Lewis. He tried to shoot the bear, but had no bullets. The bear chased him into a river, but Lewis was in luck because the bear changed its mind and went away. As you know, Lewis was very lucky. It is almost impossible to escape from a bear because bears can run very fast, swim very well, and even climb trees. Most of the Indian tribes were nice to the travelers, except for one in the mountains: the Lakota Indians. Lewis and Clark could not talk to them, but Sacagawea helped the travelers and the Lakota become friends. In many places, the river was rough, and they needed to drag the boat from the land with long ropes. When they came to rapids and waterfalls, they made a wagon to put the boat on and towed it above the falls. In the winter, they came to the Rocky Mountains, where they made a camp. They stayed in this camp for several months, until winter ended and they were able to continue. It was too cold and the snow was too deep to walk with the horses and heavy luggage. Lewis and Clark knew that the best time to cross the mountains was in the month of August. The mountains still had ice and snow in the summertime, but not so much of it. With no guides or trails, traveling was very difficult for Lewis and Clark. After a month of walking, though, they finally saw water. That was not the Pacific Ocean; the water they saw was the Columbia River.

You will be able to find this river on the map easily! At this point, Lewis again needed boats and canoes. The Indians living along the Columbia River were very friendly, so Lewis purchased several canoes from them to go down the river to the Pacific Ocean. Lewis and Clark were the first people who crossed the mountains and found their way to the Pacific Ocean. This took them almost two years. However, they traveled much faster on the way back. They traveled back in about 5 months. On their return, they stopped several times to go hunting and get fresh food. Lewis was a good hunter. One day when he went hunting with a few men, though, he got shot in the leg. That was an accident: one of his men saw his jacket made of deerskin and shot the rifle, thinking that Lewis was an animal. Fortunately, the wound was not very bad, and Lewis recovered before the expedition came back to St. Louis. Lewis and Clark took many notes for President Jefferson about the new places and different Indian tribes that they'd seen. They also looked for new animals and plants. Some of these new animals were prairie wolfs and grizzly bears. It was important for them to make good marks on the trees and big rocks with the letters "U.S." as they went. These signs meant that that land belonged to the U.S. and not to any other country. Lewis had a black Newfoundland dog named Seaman. This dog went with Lewis to the Pacific Ocean and came back to St. Louis in good health, but badly bitten by mosquitoes. In St. Louis, all of the expedition's members were welcomed as heroes. Many people had feared that they were dead. President Jefferson was very happy because he was now able to say that the U.S. territory stretched from the Atlantic to the Pacific Ocean and that the newly discovered territories belonged to the U.S.

This is just a very short story about the Lewis and Clark expedition. Many books are written about their expedition, so one day, if you want, you can read more. Didi made the story short for you.

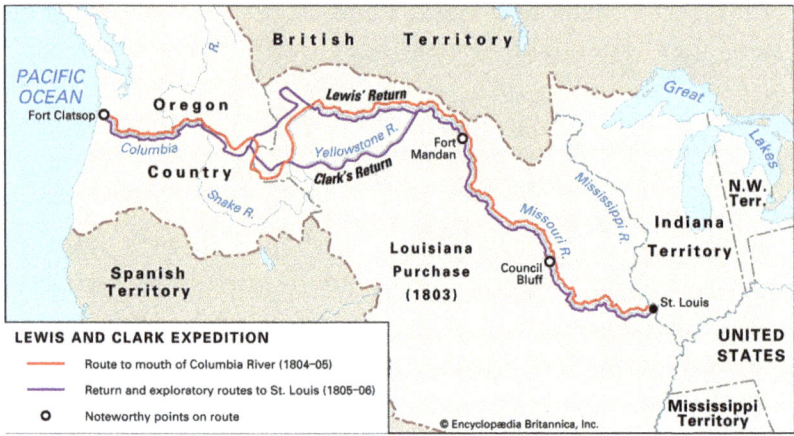

Questions:

Can you find St. Louis where the expedition started, which was a big trading town at that time?

Can you find how far they went just on the Missouri River?

Let me tell you something about hunting: it is dangerous and expensive. So why shoot animals?

GRAVITY
AND MOON

You know that Moon goes all the way around the Earth. Moon is not a planet like Saturn or Mercury; it is like a satellite that is cruising around the Earth. Moon has its gravity. Its magnetism is not as strong as the Earth's, but it does something very interesting. But before I tell you what it does, I would like to remind you of something you have already seen. When you go to the lakes or the sea to swim or play, you have noticed that the water is sometimes very low and other times much higher at the same place. We call this tide. There are low and high tides. Why is that? Where does this water come from, and where does it go every day, over and over again? The answer is, this happens because of the Moon. Moon does that to the water with its gravity. It does that to all water on the surface of our planet. When Moon is closer to your shores, Moon's gravity will pool the water up. When the same places are far from the Moon, you will see a low tide. I hope that was easy to understand. Imagine now, what would happen to a boat if a sailor left it at the pier when the tide was high. It could be on the bottom of the lake when Moon goes away and the tide becomes low. Also, kids can lose their toys on the beach if they leave them there when the tide is low. When Moon and the tide come up, the toys will float away. I am sure you can think of some other examples that could happen when tides are low and high. One day you will tell me.

MARATHON RACES

I am sure that you have heard about marathon races. There are many – in Boston, New York, Washington, and many other places all over the world. Many people run a marathon several times and often in different places. For example, girls, your mom ran three marathon races in Washington, and your father ran one in Washington with his friends from the college. This race is 26 miles long, but for some runners it's too long to make it to the finish line. Marathon races are a very popular sport, and thousands and thousands people run these races every year. Even more people watch these races on TV. Here, I need to tell you one thing. Although many people run Marathon races or hear about them and see them on TV, a lot are not sure where the word "marathon" comes from and why the race is 26 miles long. Why is this popular race called a "marathon"? And why is it 26 miles long? Well, here's the answer. As I told you last time, we will need to go to ancient Greece to get the answers to our questions. A long time ago, there were two very rich and powerful empires. One was in Greece, and the other was in Persia. Greece was in Europe, Persia was in Asia. They did not like each other, but fortunately the sea separated them, so they could not fight very often. These wars were on the land or on the sea, and the two sides had similar luck. First one side would win, but the next time, the other side would win. Greece had a much smaller army than Persia. On both sides, though, the warriors had similar weapons; swords, spears, bows and arrows, shields, and chariots with cavalry. One day, the Persian sultan (or king) decided to attack Greece. He and his army sailed from Asia to Greece on hundreds of ships with their horses and chariots. After they landed, the sultan's army started to move toward the Greek capital. Greece was ready. Although the Greeks had a smaller army, they had very well trained and brave soldiers who were ready to defend their country. They did not wait: instead, they went to meet the Persian army and push them back to the sea. These two armies met on a large field next to the city of Marathon. The fight was hard for both sides, but the Greek army came out as the winner. After a celebration in the camp, one warrior was sent from the Marathon field to the Greek capital with the good news. His name was Phillipides. The Marathon field was 26 miles away from the capital. Phillipides ran for several hours on a hot summer day. After he arrived at the capital, he told the king about the victory. Then, completely exhausted, he fell down and died. This is a true story, not mythology.

Now we know where the name Marathon comes from: a city in Greece with a field where Greece defeated the Persian army. We also know that the marathon race is always 26 miles long, which is the distance from the Marathon field to the Greek capital.

I know that you would like to ask me if I run marathon races. I like running, but it becomes boring to me after a while.

Looking at the map:

Greece is easy to find in Europe.

Today, Persia does not exist. Today, we call this country **Iran**, and you can find it in the southwest of Asia.

The Greek capital is **Athens**.

THE DEAD SEA

(and some other seas with unusual names)

Today, we will talk about geography. So far, you have learned about many interesting places, but I still have some more places to tell you about that are also interesting: for example, the seas with unusual names.

There are many seas in the world, but there is only one called the Dead Sea. It is not as big as the Mediterranean, Caribbean, or China Seas, but it is still very special.

Why it is called the Dead Sea?

The Dead Sea is "dead" because there is no life in it. There are no fish, crabs, oysters, or any other sea animals in the Dead Sea. Also, there are no sea plants in it. The Dead Sea is only water and nothing else.

Why is that?

The Dead Sea has a lot of salt in its water – about 7 times more than there is in the ocean. There is too much salt for the fish and plants to survive in this water. Since there is no life in this sea, people named it the Dead Sea.

Although the Dead Sea has no life in it and the people who live around it cannot fish, they have found other ways to enjoy it. The salted water in the sea is so thick that it's hard to swim or dive, but one can easily float on the surface of the water without fear of sinking. Floating on the surface of this water feels like lying on a couch. Many people take books or newspapers to read while floating on the surface of this sea.

The Dead Sea is not large; it is close to Jordan and Israel in West Asia.

There are some other seas with unusual names: the Black Sea, the Red Sea, the White Sea, and the Yellow Sea.

Why were they given these names?

Let us talk first about the Black and Red Seas.

A long time ago, people used the color of the water to help them navigate and get directions to the south and north. A red color was always used for south, while a black color was used for north.

Now, when we go to the map, we will find that this makes sense. The Black Sea is north of the Red Sea in West Asia.

What about the White Sea? Why it is called "white"?

The White Sea is in the north of Asia, near to North Pole. As you may expect, the name comes from the snow and ice on this sea. It is a large sea that stays white for most of the year.

We have one more sea with a funny name: the Yellow Sea.

The Yellow Sea is also in Asia. It is next to the Korean peninsula. This sea has a yellow color. The color comes from the large rivers that empty into it. These big rivers come from the deserts in central Asia and carry a lot of sand and clay, which turns the sea's water yellow.

We have now answered all of our questions about how these seas got their names. I find this interesting.

<u>And for the end, a puzzle:</u>
What year is this? MMXIV
(IV + II) x (VIII – VI) = ?

THE WEST INDIES

To My Dearest Grandsons in Maine,

This year you will visit St. John Island. There will be a lot of swimming, snorkeling, and maybe some fishing.

St. John is a small island belonging to the larger group of the West Indies. The West Indies is all continental, not volcanic islands. You may need to use a map for better orientation, but here is a diagram of how these islands are divided into groups.

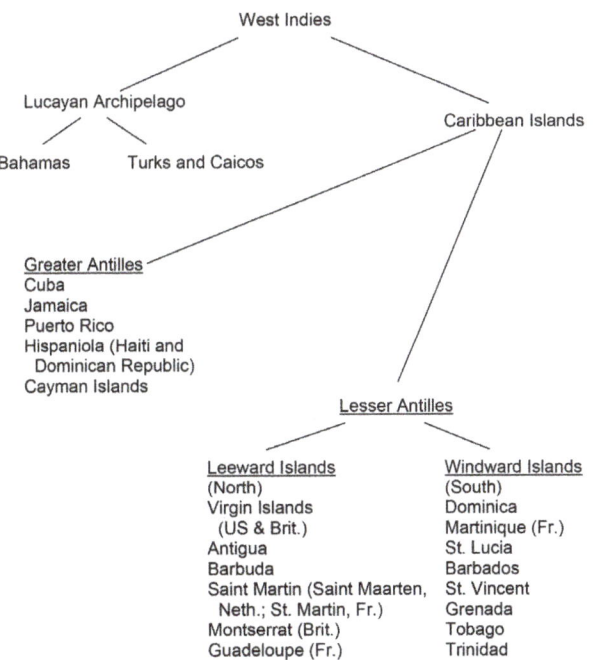

Let's try to explain some interesting things about these islands.

First, why do we call these islands the West Indies?

I know that you know the answer. But still, here's a brief reminder: Christopher Columbus, who thought that he was in India when he arrived here in 1492, named the islands the West Indies. Although we know he wasn't right, the name that he gave the islands stayed.

The West Indies consists of two groups of islands: the Lucayan Archipelago and the Caribbean islands.

Let's talk about Lucayan Archipelago first. Where does this name come from? The Lucayans were a people who lived on these islands when Columbus arrived. And *archipelago* means a line of islands. There are two groups of islands in Lucayan Archipelago: the Bahamas and the Turks and Caicos.

The Bahamas consists of more than 700 islands. Its name comes from the local "*ba ha ma*," or "big upper middle land." One of these islands is San Salvador. It was the first island that Columbus sighted and visited, on October 12, 1492. He named it *San Salvador* after Christ the Savior.

Columbus and later Spanish explorers were not interested in colonizing these small islands where they could not find gold. But later, in the eighteenth century, the British occupied the islands and brought slaves from Africa to work on their sugar plantations.

Today, the Bahamas is an independent state, and descendants of African slaves make up 90 percent of the population.

The Turks and Caicos are the other part of the Lucayan Archipelago. They are a British territory with an appointed governor. Turks Island looked to Spanish explorers like a Turkish cactus, and that's where the name comes from. The name *Caicos* originated in a local language and means "long islands."

Many people describe the Bahamas and the Turks and Caicos as Caribbean islands, but that isn't correct. They are in the Lucayan Archipelago, and we will keep them separate.

Now we move on to the Caribbean islands.

Why *Caribbean*? The Caribs were the dominant aboriginals on these islands. They arrived from South America about 4000 years ago.

The Caribbean islands are divided in to the Greater and Lesser Antilles. The name *Antilles* originated in Europe. It has a very interesting history. Before the discovery of America, it was believed in Europe that a "phantom island" lay in the Atlantic Ocean far to the west of Portugal and Spain. This island, called *Antillia*, appears on old nautical maps as a large rectangular island in Atlantic Ocean. After Columbus's discovery of America, of course, Antillia was removed from the maps, but the islands in this region came to be called, not *Antillia*, which was one island, but *Antilles*, as there were many of them.

GREATER ANTILLES

The Greater Antilles consists mostly of large islands. Most of them are sovereign states. The exceptions are Puerto Rico, which is a US territory with an elected governor and a local constitution, and the Cayman Islands, which are British territories. Each of these islands has an interesting history, but our interest right now is in the Lesser Antilles, which is your destination.

LESSER ANTILLES

The Lesser Antilles is divided in the Windward and Leeward Islands. It is interesting why they have these names. *Windward* means downwind, while *leeward* means opposite the direction of the wind. The islands were named for the prevailing winds, called the "trade winds," which helped traders navigate these seas.

The trade winds blow from the northeast to the southwest, and they helped sailors from Europe reach the Windward Islands to the south more easily than the Leeward Islands to the north. As you might expect, the Windward Islands developed better and faster than the more northern islands.

As you can see on the map, there are a lot of islands in the Antilles. Your destination is in the US Virgin Islands. The Virgin Islands are part of the Leeward Islands in the Lesser Antilles. There are three groups of Virgin Islands: British, Spanish, and US.

Columbus was the first European to visit these islands, on his second voyage to America. He gave them the fanciful name *Santa Ursula and her 11,000 Virgins*. Columbus was a Catholic and a very religious man who liked to use names from the Bible for newly discovered lands. The numerous islands here most likely reminded him of the 11,000 girls who accompanied Saint Ursula on her travels. According to legend, Ursula was a European princess who was to meet her husband along with 11,000 girls. On the way, she was captured by the Huns, a wild tribe, somewhere in Germany. All the girls were beheaded, and the Huns' leader shot Ursula dead with an arrow. Saint Ursula's name is Latin for "little bear," and her feast day is October 21 (also Dida's birthday).

Later, all these islands got a common, shorter name: the Virgin Islands. The US Virgin Islands consists of many islands, but there are three main ones: St. Croix, St. Thomas, and St. John. You will be visiting the last two. Your plane will land on St. Thomas, since St. John has no airport, and then you will take a boat to your final destination.

Again, we see that these islands have biblical names: the apostles St. Thomas and St. John. There are interesting stories about these two apostles. Saint Thomas was also called "Doubting Thomas." He was not one of the people to whom the risen Christ first appeared, and he did not believe it had happened. He asked for physical proof. Then Christ reappeared and specifically asked Thomas to touch his wounds. Later, St. Thomas traveled from the Roman Empire to India to baptize people. Pagans crucified him in India.

Saint John was luckier. He was the only one of the twelve apostles who wasn't killed while preaching Christianity. There is an interesting story about that, too. While preaching in Rome, St. John was captured, and after being persecuted was thrown into boiling oil, but he was unhurt! Afterward, he was sent to a Greek island to work in a mine, where he died of old age.

These islands were part of the Spanish Empire until 1754, when the Kingdom of Denmark took control. They imported slaves from Africa to the islands to work on sugar plantations. In 1916, Denmark sold the islands to the US for 25 million dollars.

I hope you have a lot of fun on St. John. If you go fishing, remember the joke I told you about the man who bought the largest fish in the fish market and asked to be thrown to him.

THE STORIES ABOUT THE COLONY OF VIRGINIA, JOHN SMITH AND POCAHONTAS

Now is a good time to talk about our own history. The Thanksgiving Day is coming and we like to remember what happened in our country about 400 years ago.

Since the people who came to America were from England; first, as a brief introduction, I will tell you what happen in England to force men and women to leave their homes in England.

Many years ago, King of England had a great quarrel with The Pope, the head of Catholic Church.

King Henry made up his mind and announced that he would no longer pay attention to Pope's orders. He told people in England that he, not the Pope, would be the head of the Church of England. Some people were glad of the change but some of them still took the Pope's side. King Henry died before the people became used to the change. The Church was called Anglican Protestant because it had been established as a protest to The Pope.

King Henry VIII left the throne to his daughter Mary who was an earnest Catholic. She did not like her father's ideas. Mary began at once bringing back the priests and doing everything to restore the old religion. But Mary's reign soon came to an end and Queen Elizabeth took the throne.

Elizabeth was as strong as Mary, but an English Church woman and so again the country was thrown into confusion; the churches were destroyed, priests were displaced and all who were Catholics were expected to join English Church. King James followed Queen Elizabeth.

King James was meaner than any of the Kings who had gone before him. He persecuted all, Catholic and Protestants, who did not like him.

During all this trouble in England, a group of people had been rising who believed neither in the Catholic not in the English Church. These people who hated both churches were called Puritans.

You may be sure the Puritans did not have a very enjoyable time in England under King James. Since the King was happy to get rid of these people, he gave them permission to leave England.

The Puritans went to Europe, the others unhappy people went to work for English government in America.

In 1607 a number of men went from England to America to establish and to work in the first English colony. They reached river in Virginia, which they named the James, in honor of their English King. The town they began to build they named Jamestown. One of the leading men in this company was John Smith. He was very wise and able man, and seemed always to do the right thing at just the right time. The people in the colony were all the time in danger from the Indians. On one occasion, John Smith was captured and injured by Indians; a little Indian girl saved his life and he returned back to Jamestown. Because of his injuries he for a time went to England. You would suppose that after he was gone the men in the colony would have been wise enough to keep working. But, instead, when John Smith returned to Jamestown he found the men quarreling among themselves. They had use up all provisions and were almost starving. But Smith worked hard to save Jamestown, and for a time he prevailed upon the men to stop their foolish quarreling and to go to work to build up the colony. Later they named the colony Virginia, which became an import English settlement.

Let me just tell you briefly what happened to little Indian girl, who saved life of John Smith. Her name was Pocahontas. She visited English colony many years later, she was now a young woman and was said to be very beautiful. Son of John Smith married her. That was the first marriage between the white man and Indian woman. They were very happy and had a baby boy who was as beautiful as his mother. Some of the good families in Virginia today are proud to say that they are descendants from the little son of Pocahontas.

THE MAYFLOWER AND PILGRIMS

This is what happened to the first group of people who left King James's England looking for better life in New World. These people were not Puritans; they were not trying to find a land where they could have a freedom to worship their God. Puritans are the people who went over into Holland, the country we call Netherlands this days. There they lived happily enough, but they longed for a home of their own, where they could teach their own religion and make it the religion of the country. For this reason they went back to England, obtained permission to found a colony in the new world, and with their hearts full of hope and courage, started out - in the Mayflower and the Speedwell, - for the unknown land. As you know Speedwell was too heavy with the people on the board and was obliged to put back into port. Thus it was that the Mayflower alone to sail to America.

All this happened 14 years after the group of men lead by John Smith sailed to Virginia!

You will often hear the Puritans on Mayflower, spoken of as Pilgrims. This was a name given to them because of their pilgrimages to Holland and to America in search of a home. The word "pilgrimage" means a long journey to some sacred place. Try to remember this, - these plain, honest, God-fearing people were all Puritans in England, while the few who wondered about and finally settled in Plymouth were given the name of Pilgrims.

Let us go back to Mayflower. You know the story so I will be brief.

Mayflower was bound to Virginia, never reached Virginia; because of bad weather landed on Cape Cod. It was one of those windy days that you, who live in the North Eastern States, expect to have now and then in the wintertime. The Pilgrims had intended to land much further south, where it was pleasanter and warmer; but the storm was so severe that captain of the Mayflower said he must make port wherever he could. I am afraid they were not over-pleased when the vessel came into Cape Cod harbor. The trees were leafless, the ground was frozen, and the waters about the shores were covered with the sheets of ice. But they were brave and sturdy people who went to work. These men were not idle, lazy good-for-nothings, as many of those first colonists in Virginia had been. They did not need a John Smith to urge them to be industrious. They were all terribly in earnest. They had left their native land and, with their brave wives, had come over to this wilderness to build homes for themselves.

In the fall of the following year Pilgrims were awarded, they had a great harvest and celebrated that together thanking the God on the Thanksgiving Day. Some friendly Indians jointed them.

I do not know who caught the turkey for dinner. I am sure that they had no problem because this bird is American bird, lived first only in America.

ABOUT THE ISLANDS AND THEIR PEOPLE

There are many islands on our planet, but in this brief article I will discuss what I find interesting about their peoples and histories.

It was fun to learn where the names of the islands came from. The Portuguese and Spanish explorers gave names to many islands in the Age of Discoveries. These were the times of Christopher Columbus, Ferdinand Magellan, and many other explorers who went to sea to look for new lands. Because Portugal and Spain were Catholic countries, the names given to newly discovered islands were often religious in character.

The Europeans discovered most of the islands in the Age of Discoveries, starting with the Portuguese explorers in the sixteenth century. At that time, the ruler of Portugal was Prince Henry the Navigator, who loved learning about the new lands. He developed a large flotilla before any other European rulers, and Portugal dominated the sea for almost a hundred years. Later other countries, led by Spain, Britain, and Denmark, followed the Portuguese ships and claimed the discovered lands as their own territories.

The aboriginal populations in these islands soon accepted the more advanced European lifestyle as well as European religions. Portugal and Spain used the new islands as trading posts for goods needed in Europe. The largest trading centers were in the Indian and South Pacific Oceans.

Trading over the sea was popular but not without danger. Pirates attacked the trading ships, and some made their homes on the islands of the Atlantic Ocean and the Caribbean Sea, where they hid stolen gold and jewelry.

When Portugal occupied West Africa in the sixteenth century, it started a slave trade. Many islands, especially in the Caribbean, became new trade centers. African slaves were sold to work in other countries, and some were kept on the islands to work on their plantations.

A century later, some countries, starting with Great Britain, also expelled their prisoners, criminals, and prostitutes to faraway occupied islands, including Australia and Tasmania. These were called "prison islands." Soon, though, rich farmers followed the prisoners to these islands and used them to work for free on the farms and roads. The small and remote island of St. Helena in the Atlantic became the prison of the famous French emperor Napoleon to secure Europe from his return to France.

More recently, some of these islands have become strategically important military bases. Tragically, the USA tested nuclear bombs on volcanic islands in the Pacific, and three of them were completely vaporized. Russia followed with nuclear testing and the destruction of the islands of Novaya Zemlja (New Land) in the Arctic Sea.

Some small islands are popular as banking and business centers. The best known of these are the Cayman Islands, Singapore, Cape Verde, and Hong Kong. The most beautiful islands are also popular tourist places, and for many inhabitants the tourism is the main source of income.

CONTINENTAL
AND OCEANIC ISLANDS

Before talking about individual islands, I would like to mention a few general characteristics of islands.

There are two different types of islands. *Continental islands* are connected under the sea to continents. *Oceanic islands,* or called volcanic islands, are the results of volcanic eruptions, and they are not connected to continents.

Some continental islands connected with Asia are:
Japan
Borneo
Java
Sumatra
Sri Lanka

Some continental Islands connected with Australia are:
New Guinea
Tasmania
New Zealand

Some continental Islands connected with Europe are:
Great Britain
Ireland
Sicily

Some continental Islands connected with North America are:
Greenland
Newfoundland
Long Island

Some continental Islands connected with South America are:
Barbados
Trinidad
Falklands

A continental island connected with Africa is:
Madagascar

I listed only major islands, but there are hundreds of smaller continental islands.

Oceanic islands are generally smaller than and are far away from continents. For example, St. Helena in the Atlantic Ocean and the Hawaiian islands in the Pacific are all of volcanic origin.

Let's move to a new topic: the geography of islands.

We've already talked about the West Indies, so in this review we'll go to the Atlantic first and start with the islands in the north. Then we'll continue around Africa to the Indian Ocean and visit Madagascar on the east. From there we'll sail to Sri Lanka, the island next to India. Then we'll go to Pacific Ocean, we'll start from the north again, with the Aleutian archipelago, then Japan and then the three very important islands of Taiwan, Hong Kong, and Singapore. Further out in the Pacific are the thousands of islands of the Philippines and Indonesia. We'll finish our tour with in the South Pacific with New Guinea, New Zealand, and the many small islands of Oceania. At the end, I'll tell you briefly about the Mediterranean beauties.

GREENLAND

Far north in the Atlantic Ocean is the world's largest island, Greenland, which might better be called Whiteland, since it's almost covered (75%) with ice.

The first people came to Greenland from Canada around 2500 BC and inhabited the island on and off. Norsemen (Vikings) settled in the southern part in the tenth century. It's interesting how this happened: the Norwegian-born Icelander Erik the Red was exiled to Greenland for manslaughter. After he arrived, he invited other Norwegians to join him. To make the place more attractive to newcomers, he described it as the land of green fields: Greenland. Although the settlers were disappointed, it was almost impossible for them to return home after they arrived.

These colonies disappeared in the fifteenth century. As you know, the people on Greenland left in small ships and discovered America five hundred years before Columbus, but they never stayed there long. Inuit people, the aboriginals from Canada, arrived in Greenland in the thirteenth century and remained until today.

Greenland was first ruled by the Norwegian Kingdom, but part of the island was under the Danish Kingdom, and they agreed to rule together. It stayed like that until 1300, when the Black Death (plague) hit Norway harder than Denmark. Since then Greenland, has been under the Danish Kingdom.

Today, Greenland has a population of about 50,000 and is an autonomous country of the Kingdom of Denmark. They have their own prime minister and parliament. The economy depends on fish exports. There are no roads between the cities because of the fjords; transportation is by air or boat. Two languages are spoken: Danish and Greenlandic. The people are mainly Protestant, with a Catholic minority. Unfortunately for Greenland, the country has the highest suicide rate in the world; the causes are alcoholism and unemployment.

ICELAND

Southeast of Greenland is Iceland. This island has a population of 330,000. The capital is Reykjavik. Iceland is a beautiful country with many geysers and hundreds of volcanoes, of which 30 are active.

Settlement of this island began in 875 CE with the Norwegians. They ruled until 1814. After that, Denmark took the country over and ruled until 1918, when Iceland became an independent state. Since 1944, Iceland has been a republic, with a president and a parliament.

The standard of living is high because of inexpensive geothermal and hydro power, which provide cheap heating and electricity, and good fish exports and tourism. The government pays for health services. Education is free and mandatory until age 16 (completed 94%). University is also free: there are no tuition fees, and many scholarships are available. Everything sounds very good, and the people there must be very happy.

BRITISH ISLES

Southeast of Iceland are the British Isles. There are many of these. The largest are Great Britain and Ireland, but there are about 6,000 smaller islands.

Before we talk about these islands, we need to clarify a few things that people often confuse when talking about Great Britain, Britain, England, and the United Kingdom, or UK. "Great Britain" is the name of the island. On Great Britain are three countries: England, Scotland, and Wales. The United Kingdom is a state consisting of four countries; England, Scotland, Wales, and Northern Ireland.

GREAT BRITAIN

The first people came to Great Britain from Europe 800,000 years ago, when it was still part of the continent. They were called the Celts. At the end of the Glacial Period, about 20,000 years ago, the sea levels rose and Great Britain became a separate island.

In the first century, Romans led by Julius Caesar invaded the island, and Rome governed there for about five hundred years. The Celts couldn't defend their country against the mighty Roman army and the culturally more advanced people.

After the fall of the Roman Empire in the fifth century, Germanic tribes including the Angles and the Saxons invaded Great Britain from the south. These Anglo-Saxons were former Roman mercenaries, who were invited by ruling classes in Great Britain to help their political interests. At the same time, Celts from Ireland invaded Great Britain from the north.

In the eighth century, Vikings arrived from Scandinavia. First they brutally attacked and robbed the villages and churches in the eastern part of the island, but later they became settlers and lived together with the British people.

In the tenth century, there were many small Anglo-Saxon kingdoms on the islands. These kingdoms were all unified under King Edgar the Peaceful. At that time, the societies on Great Britain were far behind those in Europe, which were more developed, educated and wealthier. This changed with William the Conqueror.

In 1066, William the Conqueror invaded the Kingdom of England from the French province of Normandy. The Normans established close connections with England, granting the aristocrats lands in both domains, but they also brought religious, political, and cultural changes. This is where the modern history of Great Britain begins.

After William Great Britain had many kings queens with many interesting stories, but we will leave those for another time. I'll just mention some brief facts: In the sixteenth century, the Kingdom of England annexed Wales. In the eighteenth century, it annexed Scotland. And in the nineteenth century, it annexed Ireland. Ireland is close to Great Britain on the map, but the people living on these two islands are only geographically close. They differ in many ways, and they are still working to resolve their disputes.

IRELAND

Ireland is politically divided into the Republic of Ireland and Northern Ireland, which is part of the United Kingdom. The population is 6.4 million.

The first humans arrived in 8000 BC by boat from Great Britain. Celtic migration from Great Britain started in the first century and continued until the seventeenth. Ireland was

Christianized in the fifth century by Catholic missionaries and St. Patrick.

After the Norman invasion in the twelfth century, England claimed rule over Ireland. This led to colonization by settlers from Great Britain, and Protestant English rule was established over the materially disadvantaged Catholic majority. When Ireland became a part the United Kingdom in 1801, about 50,000 people were sent to West Indies, and a massive immigration started and continued through Great Famine of 1845 to 1852. This disaster was caused by potato disease and the lack of English intervention.

After Ireland's war of independence in the twentieth century, the island was partitioned to create the Irish Free State (Republic of Ireland) with its capital at Dublin, and Northern Ireland with its capital at Belfast, as a part of the UK. The South is Catholic; the North is mixed Protestant and Catholic, with a Catholic majority. In Northern Ireland, there is permanent civil unrest asking for reunion with the Republic, which makes up 82% of the island. A relative peace in Ireland was established in 1990, with the Good Friday Agreement.

From these islands in the North Atlantic, we move far south to a few smaller islands. Several islands near Africa are very popular with tourists and visited by many people and boats every year: the Azores and the Canary Islands.

AZORES

These islands are Portuguese territories; their name comes from the Portuguese word for blue.

CANARY ISLANDS

This region is Spanish territory and is named after the Latin word for dogs. The first explorers here were surprised at the size of the dogs on the islands. Even today, many large dogs can be seen on the Canary Islands.

CAPE VERDE

Now we sail to an island that played an important role in the Age of Discoveries.

This region includes ten islands. Today it is independent of Portugal, but it retains Portuguese as its official language. The island's name "Verde" comes from the Portuguese for "green."

In 1494, the Pope used this island to divide the colonies and newly discovered lands between Spain and Portugal. The Treaty of Tordesillas made the meridian going through Cape Verde into a dividing line: the lands to the east of it would belong to Portugal, and those to the west to Spain. Portugal controlled Brazil, Angola, Mozambique, Africa, the Persian Gulf, India, Ceylon (Sri Lanka), and Indonesia. Spain was given everything from the Americas to the Philippines, except Brazil.

Only after the decline of the Spain and Portugal's power on the sea it was possible for other European states to colonize the territories weakly held by Lisbon and Madrid. The island used to be an important place for the slave trade. Today the island is economically one of the best countries in the world due to its banking and trade.

SAINT HELENA

South of these islands is St. Helena, which has less attractive beaches. This island is of volcanic origin. It was uninhabited when Portuguese sailors discovered it in 1502. Today it is a British territory, with a governor appointed by the United Kingdom. The economy is weak, and the country relays on the aid from Britain.

In the past, the British used this island as a prison. Its shores have high and dangerous cliffs. Napoleon Bonaparte, the French emperor, was imprisoned and died on St. Helena. (One day we will need to talk about this great warrior, who was a strategic technician of the caliber of Alexander the Great, Julius Cesar, Attila, and Hannibal.)

Members of the Zulu tribe and Boers were also sent here as war prisoners from Africa, along with many slaves from Africa, India, and Madagascar.

MADAGASCAR

Now we will leave the Atlantic and go the way of Vasco de Gamma around the Cape of Good Hope to visit the Indian Ocean. There is large island, Madagascar, to the east of Africa. This is a continental island that split from India, not Africa, about 88 million years ago.

Bantu people arrived here in 2000 BC from South East Africa, but the first settlers came by canoe from Borneo in 350 BC. When Spanish and Portuguese explorers arrived, Madagascar was a kingdom of native people, and it stayed like that until the French occupation.

Today, Madagascar is an independent democratic republic with 22 million people. The official languages are Malagasy and French. The standard of living is low: two-thirds of the population make only one dollar per day. Madagascar is the world's principal supplier of vanilla.

SRI LANKA

Sri Lanka is an island country near southeast India, with a population of 22 million people.

The first humans settled here about 120,000 years ago. Portuguese explorers later discovered island and established the city of Colombo. The Netherlands occupied the island for a time, but lost it to the British, and it remained a British colony until 1948.

The British first used the island for the production of coffee, until leaf disease destroyed the plants. Then they switched to tea, which was also very profitable. The British were hard on the local people, however, and imposed many taxes, even taxes on the possession of dogs.

The Sinhalese are the dominant ethnic group and are mainly followers of Buddhism. The Tamils are the second largest group. The speak Tamil and are followers of Hinduism. In the past, there were many frictions between the Sinhalese and Tamil people. The last civil war was in 2009, when the Tamils demanded independence. India intervened, but 40,000 Tamil civilians were killed and another 150,000 fled the island.

There are now about 77 million Tamil people around the world. They are the largest and oldest ethnic group in the modern world without a state of their own. Maybe one day they will find land on our planet to establish a home country.

The country is an independent republic today with many religions, ethnic groups, and languages. It has a good economy, with unemployment of 5% and poverty of 7%, and is among the large producers of coffee and tea. Don't forget, your aunt's family originally comes from Sri Lanka.

CHRISTMAS ISLAND

Although far from Australia in the Indian Ocean, this is an Australian territory. English explorers gave island its name because they arrived there on Christmas Eve. More recently, the island has become a place through which many asylum seekers from poor Indonesian islands try to enter Australia to find better lives.

From Indian Ocean, we will sail to the Pacific Ocean and start in the north, with a long archipelago stretching between Asia and America.

ALEUTIAN ISLANDS

The name "Aleutian" comes from a native-language word for island. There are 11 large islands and 55 small in this group, all of them volcanic islands. This archipelago goes from Alaska to Siberia, dividing the Bering Sea from the Pacific Ocean. They form a broken bridge between America to Asia, created after land was submerged by rising water during the interglacial period.

In 1741, Russians explorers, traders, and missionaries first colonized the islands. The Russian government sent Vitus Bering, a Dane, and Alexei Chirikov, a Russian, to explore North Pacific in two ships, St. Peter and St. Paul. Bering lost his life in a storm, but the survivors found the islands rich in fur-bearing animals. This triggered a flock of Siberian hunters to visit.

After the United States purchased Alaska and the surrounding islands from Russia in 1862, life on the islands improved, with the establishment of hospitals, schools, and other facilities.

The Aleutians have heavy rainfall, with about 250 rainy days every year. The temperature is low and the winds are strong year-round. The economy is based on fishing and military presence. The USA conducted its largest underground nuclear explosion in this region, and the area is still contaminated.

JAPAN

From this large group of islands, we will sail south to Japan. Japan is an island country of East Asia on a volcanic archipelago of 6,852 islands. Its population is 126 million, and the capital city is Tokyo.

Due to its location, Japan has the highest disaster risk in the world. The Japanese archipelago has 108 active volcanoes and is often exposed to destructive earthquakes that result in tsunamis several times a century.

Unlike normal ocean waves, which are generated by winds and tides, tsunamis are generated by the displacement of water, and they have far larger waves. A tsunami resembles a rapid rising tide. Any event that causes a large displacement of water, such as earthquake, volcanic eruption, underwater explosion, or meteorite impact, can cause a tsunami. The waves can be tens of meters high and carry extraordinary power. One catastrophic tsunami happened in 2004 on the day after Christmas. People call it the Christmas Tsunami. An undersea earthquake in the Indian Ocean caused a sudden vertical rise of the sea, which displaced massive volumes of water and was followed by hundred-foot high horizontal wave that advanced inland two to three miles and flattened and destroyed the land. This Tsunami killed 230,000 people in Indonesia, Sri Lanka, and Taiwan.

European traders and Christian missionaries from Portugal came to Japan for the first time in the sixteenth century. They were welcomed for bringing cultural and technical innovations, but not for long. In 1639, Japanese lords instituted a "closed country policy" that lasted two and a half centuries. They said that Christianity was destabilizing Japan and decided to prosecute it. Christian converts and missionaries were executed, and soon Christianity was eradicated in the country. After that, Japan became politically united and improved economically. In 1853 the closed country policy came to the end, and open trade was negotiated with the rest of the world.

In the past Japan fought many wars with the neighboring countries of China, Korea, and Russia. The last was World War II, which ended tragically for Japan with the explosion of two atomic bombs over the cities of Hiroshima and Nagasaki. After WWII, the country became a constitutional monarchy with an emperor and an elected parliament. A fast economic recovery followed the war due to very disciplined and hard-working people, long working hours, and loyal politicians. Today, Japan is the third major economic power in the world and a global leader in technology and machinery.

This is very short review of Japan, and many other things could be said about it. But I would like to end with a very special sport that was born in Japan: sumo wrestling.

Sumo matches are a single round and often last only a few seconds. The matches are held in a circular ring 4.55 meters in diameter. The goal is to push the other wrestler out of the ring. The Japanese like this sport, and the competitors are very popular.

Sumo wrestlers are giant men who attend special schools and training. To gain weight, they are not allowed to eat breakfast, but they eat a large lunch of meat and vegetable stew and rice, washed down with a lot of beer. After lunch there is a "siesta," a sleep break, intended to help them put on the weight. Body weight is a very important factor in their fights, but in the long term the severe obesity leads to many medical problems, such as diabetes, high blood pressure, liver disease, and arthritis.

South of Japan are three islands that are closely connected with China.

TAIWAN

In the past, this island was called Formosa, which means "beautiful" in Portuguese. The first humans arrived 20,000 years ago. About 8,000 years ago, Austronesiens migrated from Asia and absorbed the aboriginal population. The Dutch were the first Europeans to arrive, and they used the island as a trading post. In the seventeenth century, Spain built its first settlements. More and more Chinese immigrants assimilated into the population, and soon Taiwan became the part of the Chinese dynasties. In 1894, after the Sino-Japanese War, Japan ruled the country and started industrialization. Japan lost Taiwan to the Republic of China after WWII.

Taiwan has 23 million people, 95% of them Chinese, and its capital city is Taipei. Politically, it is called the Republic of China. It has high autonomy and a free economy. Its relationship with mainland China is very complicated but country remains independent territory.

HONG KONG

"Hong Kong," in Chinese, means fragrant harbor. Hong Kong is an island, but the state of Hong Kong includes also part of a Chinese peninsula and 200 surrounding islands. It has seven million people, mainly of Chinese ethnicity.

As a part of China, the country fell under several Chinese dynasties. The earliest European visitors arrived from Portugal in 1513. They received permission from China to establish trade stations in Hong Kong and Macau. In 1840, the Chinese triggered the Opium War by confiscating opium imported from India. After the war, Hong Kong became a British colony. The British occupation lasted until 1997, when Hong Kong was transferred back to China under the principle, "One country, two systems," which gives Hong Kong great autonomy. Today, Hong Kong is a major global trade and finance center.

SINGAPORE

In Chinese, *singa* means "lion" and *pore* means "city." Singapore, or "Lion City," is a country with one main island and 60 small islands located at the tip of Malaysia. The population is 5.5 million, mainly of Chinese ethnicity.

The first settlements here were built in the second century AD by local Chinese dynasties. In 1819, the British East India Company founded Singapore as a trading port. The city stayed under British control until 1963, when it became a parliamentary republic.

Today Singapore is a global commerce, finance, and transportation center that has been called "the easiest place to do business." It has effective, pragmatic, government with little corruption and fair civil services with low taxes. The government supports education. English is the language of instruction in all public schools. The country's main religion is Buddhism, with Christian and Islamic minorities.

INDONESIA

This is a country with thousands of islands (17,508), a population of 255 million, and 700 languages. Jakarta is the capital city. The name "Indonesia" comes from the Greek word "indos" meaning "Indian Island."

The first humans came to Indonesia from Taiwan around 2000 BC. Later, the country developed into Hindu and Buddhist kingdoms. It was an important trade region with China and India in the fourth and fifth centuries. The Muslim traders brought Islam in the thirteenth century, and the country remained mainly Muslim (predominantly Sunni) after that. Europeans missionaries and Portuguese traders brought Christianity during the Age of Discovery. Later, the Dutch and British arrived on these islands. The Japanese occupation during WWII was brutal, and the country ended up in Dutch control. After the Japanese surrender in 1945, Indonesia became an independent state governed by a military dictatorship with Sukarno as president. This lasted until Suharto opened the country up to foreign companies, which lead to a large economic improvement.

Today, Indonesia has the sixteenth largest economy on the world, which involves mixed private and governmental control. The country is a republic with an elected president, and the government prefers to have close relationships with its neighbors in Asia (China) more than with Europe or America.

The dominant ethnic group is Javanese (Muslim). Java is the largest island, followed by Sumatra. The island of Borneo is shared with Brunei and Malaysia, and New Guinea with Papua New Guinea. There are many smaller islands. The best known is Bali, for its beautiful beaches and famous belly dancers.

PHILIPPINES

This is an archipelago with 7,250 islands and about 100 million people. The largest island is Luzon. The capital of the state is Manila.

The aboriginal tribes of hunters and gatherers migrated to these islands about 67,000 years ago. Later, Austronesians from Taiwan brought agriculture and built the first settlements. Various kingdoms developed before the Spanish Empire took control and united the islands. At that time, Catholic missionaries converted many inhabitants and Christianity became a dominant religion.

The Portuguese explorer Magellan, working for Spain, was the first European to reach the islands, in 1521. Spanish explorers named them the *Philippines* in 1542 in honor of King Phillip II of Spain. In 1896, the Philippines were ceded to the US for a compensation of $20 million. The US refused to recognize the Philippine government, which started the Philippine-American War.

In 1946, the Philippines became independent, and today it has a democratic government. It is a multiethnic country, with significant Muslim and Chinese groups that were suppressed during the three-hundred-year Spanish occupation.

NEW GUINEA

This island is the second largest after Greenland. After the glacial period ended, Australia and New Guinea were separated by the Torres Strait. Human presence on the island dates to about 50,000 BC, beginning with migration out of Africa. Portugal and Spain first discovered the island and named them for the people's similar appearance to the natives of Guinea in Africa.

Politically, the islands is divided between the east, which is Indonesian, and the west, which is an independent country but was previously Australian. The islands have thousands of tribal groups speaking 1,073 languages.

NEW ZEALAND

Between sixty and eighty-five million years ago, the continent of Zealandia broke away from Australia. The non-submerged part of the continent is New Zealand, southeast of Australia. It consists of North and South Islands. It was the last island settled by humans. The Polynesians settled on it in 1300 AC and developed Maori culture.

Tasman, a Dutch explorer, was the first European to reach New Zealand. He named it for Zealand, the province of small islands in the Netherlands. James Cook mapped the islands in 1769, and in 1840 New Zealand became a British colony. Many Maori were enslaved and died from infection by settlers' diseases.

Today, the population is 4.5 million, mostly from European ethnic groups. The country exports wine and meat. The capital is Wellington on North Island, named by the Duke of Wellington, who defeated the strategic genius Napoleon Bonaparte of France at the Battle of Waterloo. Although Napoleon's strategy in this battle was superior, he lost because the one of his generals was a joke who could not make the right decisions.

TASMANIA

This island is south of Australia. It was separated from Australia about 10,000 years ago, when the sea rose. The Dutch explorer Abel Tasman named the island.

Before British colonization in the 1800s, Tasmania was occupied by the aboriginals, who were later wiped out by British settlers and their infectious diseases. Tasmania became one of the first British prison islands. About 65,000 convicts were sent from throughout the British Empire to Tasmania to build the first colonies. Wealthy middle-class settlers began arriving in large numbers after 1820. The British government promised them the land and free convict labor.

Tasmania has a cool climate; in the summer, the average temperature is 70 F.

OCEANIA

Oceania consists of Melanesia, Micronesia, and Polynesia. Most of these islands are volcanic, except New Zealand. The islands of Oceania are oceanic or volcanic islands and are part of the Ring of Fire, a horseshoe-shaped line of volcanoes that follows the coasts of Asia and America. The name comes from the fire created from volcanic eruptions of lava.

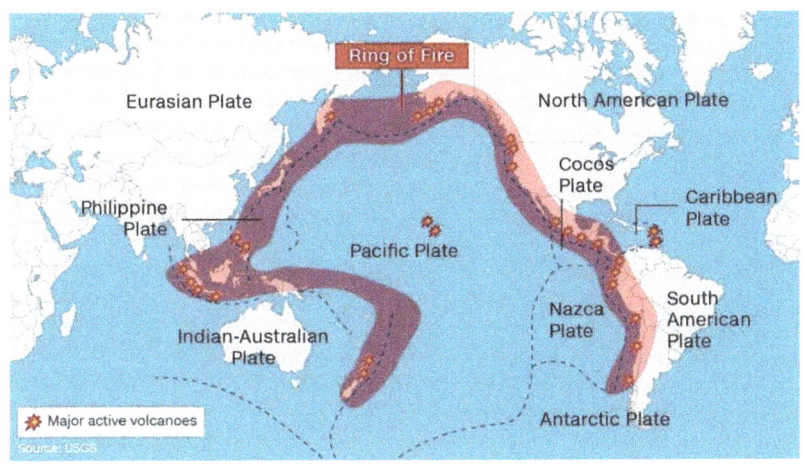

POLYNESIA

The islands within the triangle formed by Hawaii, New Zealand, and Easter Island make up Polynesia, with Tahiti and Samoa in the center. These islands are the territories of different countries. The US claims Hawaii and American Samoa. The British claim Pitcairn Island. New Zealand claims Niue and Tokelau.

Chile claims Easter Island (or Rapa Nui). This island was named by Dutch explorers, who discovered it on Easter. It is famous for its 887 monumental statues, remnants of the island's aboriginal culture.

France claims French Polynesia (Tahiti, the Society Islands, and Bora Bora). James Cook named Society Islands, as they lie contiguous to one other.

The population of Polynesia is from the Austronesian people. All the Polynesian Islands suffered a great population decline due to endemic diseases carried by Western explorers (smallpox, measles, and tuberculosis). The main religion is Christianity, as a result of missionary work. The economy depends on tourism.

Polynesian society is mainly matrilinear. A matrilinear system identifies people by their mother's lineage for family name, inheritance, titles, and so on. Although this system has been changing recently, on most islands the mother is still the dominant figure in the family. Many other societies have similar systems For example, in North America matrilinearity was followed in the Cherokee, Navajo, and Iroquois tribes. In some population groups in India and China, the Basques in Spain and France, and most Jewish communities, the families acknowledge the mother's lineage. Can you imagine being called Nick or Luka Banovac, by your mother's maiden name?

MICRONESIA

The name of this region comes from the Greek *micros*, meaning small, and *nisos*, meaning island. It has four main archipelagos: the Carolina Islands, the Gilbert Islands, the Mariana Islands, and the Marshal Islands, totaling about 2,100 islands. Most of islands are the part of a coral atoll. Coral atolls begin as corals growing on the slopes of a volcano. When the volcano sinks, the coral continues to grow, keeping the reef at or above water level.

Ferdinand Magellan was the first European to reach these islands. On his trip around the world, he stopped with his four ships at Mariana Islands to get fresh food. Here he met unfriendly people who boarded his ships and stole whatever they could. Magellan attacked them and burned several villages, but during the mission he was fatally wounded. The Spanish navigators who came to the islands later named them after the Spanish Queen Mariana of Austria.

Micronesia shares a history with Polynesia and Melanesia. It is divided politically into several independent countries, along with territories of the United Kingdom and the US. The Mariana

Islands, the Wake Islands, and Guam are US territories. The economy is based on the tourism, fishing, and grants from the US.

During the Cold War, the American military performed more than seventy nuclear tests in this area, including the explosion of a hydrogen bomb. These tests vaporized three coral islands. The surrounding islands were evacuated and have never been repopulated. The US government is still providing financial compensation to their unhappy people.

In the Marshal Islands, there is a group of islands called Bikini. These islands are popular touristic destinations with beautiful beaches. The French fashion designer Reard was impressed with the beauty of the Bikini islands named his new swimsuit design a "bikini" in the hope that its revealing style would create a commercial and cultural sensation similar to the 1946 nuclear explosion at Bikini Atoll. I think he was right: bikini swimsuits cover very little from the sun and remain very popular.

MELANESIA

The name of these islands comes from the Greek *melos*, for black. The people on these islands are a distinct ethnic group from those of Polynesia and Micronesia. They are dark-skinned, and 10% of them have bright blond hair.

The region contains four independent countries: Vanuatu, the Solomon Islands, Fiji, and Papua New Guinea. Some of the islands are under Indonesian government, and New Caledonia is a French territory.

Captain James Cook named New Caledonia because the purple hills reminded him of Caledonia in his homeland and the Scottish Highlands covered with beautiful purple heather.

The Solomon Islands got their name from Spanish explorers in sixteenth century. They found sand gold in the mud and believed they had found the source of King Solomon's wealth.

In many islands in this region, but especially in Melanesia, tattooing is very common. The women more than the men get tattoos all over their bodies. It is said that these tattoos were supposed to impress the opposite sex and scare enemies.

There is an interesting myth about how the tattooing tradition started. After an argument at home, a wife left her husband and went to her father's house. Unhappy, the husband followed and saw her father painting his house in different colors. He asked his father-in-law to paint him too, to be better looking. The paint was washed away after the rain so he went back and asked him to make permanent colors. After the tattooing was finished, the nicely decorated husband fascinated his wife, who gladly came back. As a doctor, though, I can say that our skin does not like tattoos.

With this little story we complete our travels through Oceania. We still have another group of islands with interesting histories and peoples, though. These are in the Mediterranean Sea. The largest islands there are Cyprus, Crete, Sicily, Sardinia, and Corsica.

CYPRUS

The fist humans on Cyprus arrived in 10,000 BC. The Greeks settled here in 2000 BC. After this, the island became strategically important and was ruled by many groups. In order, these were the Assyrians, Egyptians, and Persians, Alexander the Great, the Roman Empire, the Arab caliphates, the Venetians, and finally the Ottoman Empire. In 1878, Cyprus was placed under British administration, but today it is an island country divided into two parts. The Republic of Cyprus is a Greek region, and the northern part of island is Turkish territory, and as the self-declared Turkish Republic of North Cyprus. The long-lasting territorial dispute between Greece and Turkey is still unresolved.

The ancient Greeks loved this island and gave it an important place in their mythology. Their goddess of love and beauty, Aphrodite, was born there. There are many stories about this beautiful woman but I like the following one a lot.

On this island, a baby boy named Adonis was born, and Aphrodite fell in love with him after being wounded by Cupid's arrow. (I'm sure you remember this young fellow, who shot his golden arrow all over the place to make people happy.) Aphrodite gave the baby to Persephone to take care of. (You remember her too: she spent half the year with her husband Pluto in the Underworld and half with mother on the Earth.) Persephone was also taken by Adonis' beauty refused to give him back. The dispute between the goddess was settled by Zeus, (the Romans called him Jupiter): Adonis was to spend a third of the every year with each goddess and the last third wherever he chose; he chose to spend it with Aphrodite. A third goddess also liked the handsome Adonis; she was Artemis, the goddess of war and hunting. Out of jealousy, she sent a wild bear to kill Adonis, and he died in Aphrodite's arms. She was very sorry, so to remember him she sprinkled his blood with nectar, from which sprang a short-lived flower, the anemone.

Cyprus has beautiful cypress trees, which the island's name comes from. I am not sure whether Cyprus has Aphrodite's short-lived anemones. Maybe there are some, but we know that in mythology everything is possible.

CRETE

Crete is another island mentioned in Greek mythology. The gods Zeus and Apollo and the goddess Artemis was said to be born on this island. It is also where Theseus killed the Minotaur in the Labyrinth, and Icarus and his father Daedalus were imprisoned and made wings to escape the island. Crete was the center of the earliest civilization in Europe and has been ruled by various empires, like Cyprus.

Crete has a population of about 600,000. Its economy is based on vine production, the export of olives, oranges, and citrons, and tourism. Many visitors are attracted to the numerous archeological sites from the Minoan Era. They also like to hear that Crete is free of dangerous animals like snakes. The ancient Greek attributed that fact to the labor of the hero Hercules, who first removed the dangerous Cretan bull to the peninsula of Peloponnesus, and then to honor the birthplace of the god Zeus, cleared the island of harmful and poisonous animals.

Speaking of its animals, it is interesting to note that about 800,000 years ago, there were many dwarf animals on Crete, including dwarf elephants, deer, and hippopotamuses. This often happens when large animals colonize small places like islands and evolve into smaller forms, most likely due to the shortage of food.

SICILY

Sicily is now an autonomous region of Italy, but in the past it was a colony of the Phoenicians and the Greeks, and after the fall of the Roman Empire it fell under various other rulers: the Vandals, Ostrogoths, Byzantines, Arabs, Normans, and Spanish. In 1860 the island became part of Italy.

Around 750 BC, the Greeks settled Sicily. The native Sicini people were rapidly absorbed by the superior Greek culture. At the same time, a small part of the island was colonized by Carthage, at that time the strongest power in the Mediterranean. This led to a long-lasting territorial dispute between the Greeks and Carthage, which started the Punic Wars.

Briefly, there were three Punic Wars that lasted almost a hundred years. In the first, the Greeks on the island were afraid that they might lose and made peace with the Roman Republic. After the Roman army intervened, Carthage's forces were crushed. In the Second Punic War, Carthage returned much stronger and led by the famous general Hannibal. You will remember that he crossed the Alps with elephants, and after several victories on the way reached the gates of Rome. The scared Romans shouted "Hannibal ante portas" (Hannibal outside the door), and we still say this when something or someone is in danger. But Hannibal urgently needed to return home to defend his country from other enemies, and the Roman Republic was saved from likely a severe defeat. The Third Punic War, however, ended Carthage forever. The Roman general Scipio defeated Carthage, burned the city, and sold the people into slavery. You may remember that Scipio used trumpets to panic the elephants, which led to his victory.

Sicily is also home to Mount Etna, the tallest active volcano in Europe. There is a Greek legend about Etna. Typhon, a monster of enormous strength, was said to have been born here. As an adult, Typhon liked neither liked gods nor men. One day, he challenged Zeus for the rule of the cosmos, but Zeus overcame him easily. The defeated Typhon was buried under Mount Etna and is the cause of its eruption and earthquakes.

SARDINIA AND CORSICA

There are two islands in the Mediterranean north of Sicily. Sardinia is part of Italy, and Corsica is part of France. As you might expect, these neighbors had very similar histories. They both had a variety of rulers: Carthage, Greece, the Roman Republic, the Vandals, the Ostrogoths, the Lombards, and the Kingdom of Spain.

The French emperor Napoleon Bonaparte was born in Corsica in 1769. You might expect that when he became the ruler of France, the island would prosper, but Napoleon neglected Corsica. He could never forget that when he was a young military officer supporting the French Revolution, he and his family were expelled from the island.

Another interesting thing about Corsica is that it is the birthplace of *vendetta*. The rules of vendetta required deadly revenge for offences against a family's honor. This Corsican brutality does not exist anymore, but thousands of people died on the island defending the honor of their families.

Corsica has relatively small economy based mainly on tourism. In the past, many attempts were made to enrich the island's agriculture, and one governor ordered all farmers and landowners to plant four trees every year: a chestnut, an olive, a fig, and a mulberry tree.

With these two islands we complete our visit to the Mediterranean.

We have talked about many islands and many interesting facts about them, not only about their geography. This was mixed with discoveries, mythology, wars, history, and interesting peoples and exotic customs, making them interesting and easier to remember. We also covered a lot of our planet's surface, with a lot of fascinating places and interesting people on different continents. Maybe one day I'll write about continents and their people for you. I love my enthusiastic young readers too much, and I always try to find the energy and time to write stories for them.

www.ingramcontent.com/pod-product-compliance
Lightning Source LLC
Chambersburg PA
CBHW051208120626
46547CB00013B/1263